Sisters of the Good Shepherd

Practical Rules For The Use Of The Religious Good

Sisters of the Good Shepherd

Practical Rules For The Use Of The Religious Good

ISBN/EAN: 9783742861702

Manufactured in Europe, USA, Canada, Australia, Japa

Cover: Foto ©ninafisch / pixelio.de

Manufactured and distributed by brebook publishing software (www.brebook.com)

Sisters of the Good Shepherd

Practical Rules For The Use Of The Religious Good

PRACTICAL RULES

FOR THE USE OF

The Religious of the Good Shepherd

FOR

THE DIRECTION OF THE CLASSES

> « *Instruct yourselves thoroughly in all that relates to the Institute, even in the smallest things. Be very attentive, gathering, grain by grain, like little birds, the spiritual food which is given you.* »
> (*Inst.*, ch. III.)

ANGERS, LECOQ

1898

Letter of our very honored Mother Mary of Saint Marine

My very dear daughters,

When placing in your hands this little book of *Practical Rules,* dictated by experience, I feel urged to say, Study it. In it you will find the teachings of our Venerable Mother Foundress whose heart, overflowing with charity, was consumed with love for God and souls. Conform to the rules it contains, so that being conducted according to the same spirit our Institute may respond to the exhortation of the Apostle Saint Paul. — « Fulfil ye my joy that you be one mind having the same charity, being of one accord, agreeing in sentiment. »

It is especially to you, young branches ingrafted by the Good Shepherd on the tree of the Institute, that we say — study, meditate, engrave on your hearts the means indicated to help you to realize the end of the sublime vocation bestowed on you; try to be throughout life, useful religious who procure the glory of God by giving Him souls.

Our Venerable Mother Foundress, repeated often when showing us the greatness of our mission, « Love your vocation, my dear daughters, love its works. » And I mingling my voice with hers, say to you, Love your vocation, it is that of Jesus; love its works, they are those of Jesus. With Him, cherish the child whose young soul requires your religious solicitude to incline it to receive the influence of grace and learn to know and love its Creator. Leave nothing undone to form it to the practice of Christian virtues, and thus you will assure its happiness in this life and in the next. With Jesus, love above all the stray sheep whom He seeks and loves to lead back to the fold. Guide yourselves by sentiments of tenderness, love, and mercy, drawn from the Heart of that good Pastor who said that He did not come for the just but for sinners.

Only in heaven, my dear daughters, will be understood the beauty and grandeur of your vocation; but the more we shall have loved it here below, and the more holily we shall have fulfilled its obligations, the more clearly heaven will reveal to us its mystery.

After having, with our Venerable Mother, excited you to love your vocation, we must also repeat with her, my dear daughters, « Love its spirit which is pre-eminently a spirit of obedience and abnegation. »

Be then true Religious, observe faithfully your Rule, keep carefully your holy Vows and respond fully to the invitation of the divine Master. « Let him who will be my desciple, renounce himself, take up his cross and follow me. »

Is it not specially to us Religious of the Good Shepherd that this call is addressed? The holy ambition to gain souls to Him, has enrolled us under His standard. Do not think, my dear daughters, that we will reach our end by any other way than the one He has Himself marked out for us. Following Him we must carry our cross, let ourselves be nailed to it, and like Him die on it, if such be His good pleasure, for the souls He has confided to us.

It is by meditating on your Rules and the Constitutions of our holy Order, by reading the *Instructions* of our Venerable Foundress, and by imprinting on your minds the counsels contained in this little book, that you will learn to be charitable auxiliaries of Him who has said. « I am the Good Shepherd. The Good Shepherd gives his life for His sheep. »

My dear daughters — you who have already laboured long years in the field of the Father of the family, you who are commencing your career and have only quitted the cradle of your religious infancy, and you also dear novices, hope of the Institute — may you respond to the ardent desire of my heart! May you be throughout the world in every part of the globe where you are placed or may be placed by holy obedience, faithful Shepherdesses of the Lord! Be careful to preserve the tender lambs from the tooth of the ravaging wolf; be strong to snatch from him the prey he has already seized; be perfect in order to conduct your flocks *by justice and kindness* to the heavenly pastures to which they are invited by the heavenly Pastor! Such ought you to be my dear daughters to fulfil the promises you have made to the Lord.

When in the midst of your labours, trials and sorrows shall oppress your heart, when the cross shall weigh upon your shoulders, when nails pierce your feet and hands, then be glad and rejoice, for by these days of suffering you will purchase from God conversions and pardons which are the object of your fourth Vow.

May our Venerable Mother Foundress and all the holy souls who have shared her noble labours, obtain for you, my dear daughters, from the Heart of Jesus, a perfect understanding of your holy vocation and excite in you the sincere and efficacious desire of sacrificing yourselves until death for the sublime work to which He has called you!

I have every hope that my wishes will be fulfilled, and I beg the holy Hearts of Jesus and Mary to bestow on you, my dear daughters, and on all the Institute, their most abundant benedictions.

Sister Mary of Saint Marine Verger,
Superioress General.

Angers, April 24th 1897.

PREFACE

This book has not been undertaken to propose new practices, but to assure the observance of those which have been transmitted, for more than sixty years, in our Congregation. Example instructs better than precept, and that of the ancient religious is of more value to their Sisters than any book; but examples are more quickly remarked, they are more touching and more easily remembered, when we read the precepts and seek to penetrate them.

What a pity our Venerable Mother Foundress did not herself write these Practical Rules which she observed in such a perfect degree, with such profit to souls, and which she taught to the Sisters formed under her direction! However, all her instructions have not been lost! many of them are still preserved in her conferences, exactly as they were delivered. We have sought with pious care all the passages which contain, properly speaking, practical rules, and these quotations from the Book of Conferences, form a considerable portion of the present work.

As to the rest, we may say that her spirit which, God be blessed, has not ceased to reign in the Institute, will be found in it. If any young Sister be surprised at seeing here or there a recommendation painful to nature, it is a sign that she has not yet learned to cultivate in herself the spirit of faith, the spirit of zeal, and the love of sacrifice which animated the Venerable Mother Mary of Saint Euphrasie Pelletier, or that she does not sufficiently share her ambition to govern by justice and kindness.

We may well apply to these rules the sweet words by which she terminates the *fiftieth chapter of her* Conferences, « *A Mistress who will be faithful to all these recommendations, who will try to put in practice all that we have said, may be sure she has accomplished her mission. Oh! she will be the cherished daughter of my heart and will have a right to my most tender affection!* »

In these pages it will be seen that we have tried as much as possible to foresee the details which may be met with in practice. Of course all could not be foreseen. The cases that may present themselves are innumerable and of infinite variety. Sometimes it is most important to adopt in two cases seemingly alike, a line of action quite different. A good decision is an affair of judgment; each person must reflect. A collection of rules may direct reflection, but cannot supply for it. « *Have discernement* » *said our Venerable Mother.*

A young religious will then not content herself with reflecting on this book; she will religiously observe the conduct of her seniors, particularly those who succeed best in their employments and who show in their words and conduct, the best spirit; she will often ask them to explain the motives of their actions. Above all, she will ask the Holy Ghost to deign to direct her Himself and to conduct her in the ways of wisdom and prudence.

Our Sisters will understand that the recommendations contained in this little Book are not all positive rules.

They must discern between the essential directions for the treatment and government of the classes, and recommendations of minor importance, which may vary with countries and circumstances. The Superioress of each house should decide those small matters.

CHAPTER I

Zeal

« All religious Institutions have a particular end. Our particular office as Religious of the Good Shepherd, our vocation, is not to save and sanctify ourselves alone, it is also to labour for the sanctification of others.

« Our vocation is a vocation of zeal, an apostolate of charity, we must reflect that our whole life ought to be consecrated to the propagation of the holy faith and to the sanctification of souls. We must form hearts and in order to form them we must instruct them... In this manner we will accomplish our fourth vow which may be said to be the essence of our vocation, the other three should be regulated in a manner to refer to it as the supreme end of our Congregation.

« You may say that there is a contract passed between you and Mary from the day of your entry into this Institute of Our Lady of Charity of the Good Shepherd. You on your side have taken the engagement to labour in a special manner for the conversion of sinners, and Mary on her side, to cover you with a special protection as long as you are faithful to the obligations you have contracted. » *(Inst.,* ch. II.)

« The object of our thoughts, our desires, our words, and our actions, ought to be the salvation of our dear sheep, after the example of our Divine Saviour whose thoughts desires and labours had no other end. Be full of holy zeal to save the poor souls confided to your care. Let this be the occupation of your life. Let this thought follow you in your prayers to render them more fervent, in your communions to animate them with the holiest affections, in the fulfilment of your duties to inflame you more and more with the fire of charity and zeal. Render yourselves worthy of your sublime vocation, by an ardent, active, vigilant zeal, and a boundless charity always taking the Shepherd of shepherds as a model.

« Labour to strengthen those who are weak, to cure those who are sick, to bind the wounds of those who are hurt. Raise those who are fallen seek those who are lost. *(Inst.,* ch. VI.)

« Have a pure persevering zeal not an unstable capricious zeal which lasts for weeks and then falls off, but a daily, unwavering zeal, which recognizes no difference of persons or country. An enlightened zeal which will save us from falling into acts of imprudence even under an appearance of good. Let us seek counsel when we are in doubt. A want of prudence often leads us into unpardonable follies. *(Inst.. ch.* LIII.)

« See how in the world each one strives to make himself perfect in his calling. Men of letters, merchants, artists, all endeavor to excel in their special vocation. If you speak to a sister of charity you will see that her thoughts are full only of wounds to be healed, of sick to be cured. If you speak to a Carmelite you will see that she will talk of St Teresa and that she thinks only of St Teresa; and our only thought should be the salvation of our brethren. *(Inst.,* ch. XXVI.)

« Oh, my God! what do we in this world, and why are we here, if we do not contribute to the salvation of our brethren? » *(Inst.,* ch. IV.)

CHAPTER II

Our own sanctification

A religious of the Good Shepherd who would be worthy of her vocation should apply herself in the first place with great ardor to the work of her own sanctification. « To work usefully for the sanctification of souls, you must be holy, you must belong all to God, and not think any more of yourself or of creatures. » (*Inst.*, ch. vi.)

« You must endeavour to raise your soul to the height of the vocation which God has given you. Your thoughts, your sentiments, your affections, must be the thoughts, the sentiments, the affections of the saints and of Jesus Christ himself. Your virtue must not be an ordinary and common virtue; you must endeavour to attain the highest degree of perfection. » (*Inst.*, ch. xxxv.)

« Have first of all, charity for yourselves that is an ardent zeal for your spiritual advancement : otherwise it will not be possible for you to have true charity, true zeal for the souls confided to you, and whom you must feed from the superabundant charity of your own heart. Oh! be very generous my children!

« Do not be in the vineyard of the Lord without the necessary tools for your work; He will dismiss you as inefficient labourers. » *(Inst.*, ch. LIII.)

A religious of the Good Shepherd is the canal by which the waters of grace flow to the souls which are confided to her. If the canal be obstructed by her faults, how will the waters pass? If it be pierced by her lightness, how will it reach the souls? She ought to be then a model [1] for the children, she ought to live by faith, practise humility, devotion, and charity, and have a true spirit of sacrifice.

Faith. — « Our Institute is an Institute of faith and love. A religious possessed of lively faith sees God everywhere and in all things, therefore her obedience is perfect. Her mind,

---

[1] Zeal does not consist properly speaking, in always preaching, in giving good advice, in continually exhorting, but rather in giving good example. Example makes a much deeper impression than words. (Inst., ch. LIII.)

her spirit, her will, all submit. The way of faith is the way of the cross; a spouse of our Lord Jesus Christ, who lives by faith will be always contented, whatever tribulation she endures, whatever contradictions she experiences in the employment assigned her; for she is happy to have something to offer to God, and flies to his bosom. » *(Inst.,* ch. v.)

Humility. — « Our vocation requires humility, annihilation of self. Each one should consider herself as the last in the community. In this way we gain souls to God. » *(Inst.,* ch. VII.)

« Oh! my daughters, if you were truly humble you would be precious religious, you would be gold and silver vessels. By humility you prepare yourselves to go to the conquest of souls. By the acquisition of this virtue you render yourselves worthy to be so many missionaries. Those amongst you who seem possessed only of moderate talent, are, nevertheless, if humble, capable of all things, with God's assistance. Then love humility, love to be unimportant, love to be forgotten. Unite with the sentiments of your own misery, unlimited confidence in God's goodness, you will be strong in the very strength of God, and you will daily increase in intimate union with Him. » *(Inst.,* ch. XVIII.)

Charity. — « When love is ardent, it is called zeal; therefore zeal is nothing else than love. Consequently, as is love, so is zeal. If love is good; zeal is good, it love is bad, zeal is bad. » (St Francis of Sales. *Treatise on the love of God.* l. X, ch. xii.)

Sacrifice. — We must never forget that sacrifice is the great means of saving souls; our Lord has taught us no other. A mistress must then be disposed to endure for her children all the sufferings it shall please our Lord to send her; she shall even have the courage to impose some on herself sometimes. She must die to herself, suffer without complaining, and never show weariness or disgust for being with the children.

« A religious of the Good Shepherd should never say : « I cannot accustom myself to this place, or, another office would suit me better. » If love for the cross, desires for suffering and self-denial, were lacking in the Institute, it would be on the verge of perishing. » *(Inst.,* ch. iv.)

« The eternal salvation of souls is indeed worth a few years of suffering. » *(Inst.,* ch. xxv.)

« A pusillanimous religious who loves her own ease too much, who flies fatigue or contradictions, is not capable to work for the conquest of souls; she is too small too narrow minded in everything.

« A novice, without the spirit of sacrifice though endowed with the finest qualities of mind, is capable of but little service and becomes a burden rather than an assistance in a community. Oh, how baneful is self love when it predominates in a soul. » *(Inst., ch. xx.)*

« A mistress who has not true and solid piety can do no good with the penitents. » *(Inst., ch. III.)*

« What should you not do to perfect yourselves in the practice of your holy interior exercises; of prayer, of communion, and pious reading of the office, of examination of conscience, in a word, of all your spiritual exercises. Prepare your souls for them by constant recollection, and beware of letting yourselves become distracted by the wanderings of your imagination.

« Do not forget this maxim of the saints, which I have cited to you several times : If you neglect prayer, if you do not assiduously cultivate it, it will take you a day to accomplish what you might do in an hour, and your work, moreover, will leave much to be desired. » *(Inst., ch. xxvi.)*

« Be very ardent and very zealous, my dear children, for the salvation of souls, and to this end be devoted to prayer and holy communion; for, where will you find the necessary graces to faithfully fulfil your missons if not from the Author of all grace. The evil one knows how to use his batteries to the best advantage. He knows that a religious without prayer has no longer strength to labour for the salvation of souls; that is why he adroitly tries to turn us from it.

« If you wish to meditate well fly dissipation and be humble.

« Never, my dear daughters, never will you labour efficaciously for the salvation of souls, if you have not first sought in prayer and silence the light necessary for this end. Religious animated with the spirit of God effect many more conversions than religious endowed with great talents, and who speak with fluent grace. » *(Inst.*, ch. XIII.)

CHAPTER III

To pray for our children

The conversion of sinners is above all the work of God; it is on God we must count, it is God we must call to our aid. He will never refuse to help a soul who is faithful to Him. We must recur to Him by prayer, recommending to Him all we undertake for His glory, acting always in concert and in union with Him [1]. We must above all invoke Him in difficult circumstances.

« These poor children, slaves of their passions await their deliverance from your prayers and mortifications, for, our Lord tells us that there is a kind of devil that is not cast out but by prayer and fasting. » *(Inst.*, ch. XXVIII.)

« Oh how wise our venerable Institutor was

---

[1] Let us go before the Tabernacle to weep not only for our own sins but also for those of the sheep confided to our care. (Inst., ch. XII.)

in recommending us to implore the Sacred Hearts of Jesus and Mary for light to know how to treat our penitents! In our Book of Customs we read : They should frequently ask the Divine Heart of Jesus the source of all sanctity, to grant them the virtues of prudence and gentleness bearing in mind that these souls have not been redeemed as St Peter says, by gold and silver but by the precious blood of Jesus Christ. » *(Inst.,* ch. XLIX.)

« How beautiful is your mission, my beloved children! And how necessary is prayer to fulfil it well! Each of you must offer for this intention all her sacrifices, all her mortifications, all her good works; and thus every moment of our lives will be consecrated to the salvation of these dear souls. A spirit of charity should impel you to work without ceasing. In the recitation of the Office, in your singing, in your work, you ought only to have in view to glorify God and to procure the good of souls. Oh! how I rejoice when I hear you all singing the sacred offices, above all on feast days; it gives me such a devotion that I could almost cry with joy. I believe your piety and fervour serve much for the conversion of souls. » *(Inst.,* ch. LII.)

It would be an excellent practice for a Mistress to propose in each of her communions to obtain from our Lord the conversion or perseverance of a child; by this means she would, in the first place avoid the danger of a tepid communion; she would maintain herself in the true spirit of her vocation and draw down on her class the most precious benedictions.

We should also call to our assistance the Blessed Virgin and our Angel Guardian and the Angel Guardians of the children.

« Those who pray and those who, instead of prayer offer their labour to God, as all who are employed in the most laborious works of the house can do, even the sick on their bed of suffering, often labour more efficaciously for the salvation of souls than they who are charged with the classes.

« Perhaps she who has the humblest office among us and attracts least attention, is the one who, by the ardour of her good desires, obtains the conversion of souls, while others who seem to have all the merit of these works, may sometimes have but a very small share. » (*Inst.*, ch. LII.)

CHAPTER IV

Religious Instructions

« Know that the great means of laboring for the salvation of souls and the conversion of sinners is to instruct them in the truths of their faith, and to deeply imprint these truths in their hearts, to teach them the catechism, to explain to them the maxims of the Gospel for it is the only road to christian sanctity.

« Apply yourselves then my dear daughters to the study of religion, that you may become good mistresses to your children. I cannot recommend too much the study of the catechism. It is a book we should always have in our hands.

« Read frequently Sacred History and particularly the History of the Church. Such reading will afford you much matter for the instructions you shall have to give to your classes. You will edify your children; they shall hear you with pleasure, and you will do them good.

« Therefore neglect nothing in your religious instructions my dear daughters.

« The salvation of one who is ignorant may be said to be more in danger than that of one who is well instructed. One who is instructed may finally yield to the voice of its conscience, may heed its remorse. But what hope is there of converting a poor ignorant creature who has never heard of God, who does not know what vice or virtue is? » (*Inst.*, ch. II.)

It is desirable that the *text* of the catechism be engraven on the memory of all our children. In the classes where the custom of reciting it is established it should be continued and where this custom does not exist it would be well to introduce it, if that can be conveniently done.

However we should not force the children who have learned another catechism to recite the one we use if they find it too difficult. « Some are not capable of learning the catechism word for word and if we exact it rigorously they will feel humiliated and discouraged. » (*Inst.*, ch. L.)

The little girls who receive lessons should be obliged to learn Sacred History. This study so neglected in our days should take precedence of all others. We would not wish a person who had passed her childhood in our house to be less advanced in secular knowledge than the children of public schools, still more should we blush if she were ignorant of Sacred History.

It is necessary to explain *the very words of the catechism,* giving the sense of them in a precise manner.

In order the better to fix the explanations in the memory, it is good to appeal to the intelligence of the children and habituate them to seek and find out the sense of the words by comparing them to other similar words. For instance in the *Christian doctrine,* show them the relation between *Christ* and *Christian doctor* and *doctrine.* We may also ask them to find words having exactly or nearly the same sense and which are clearer for them as *Teachings given by our Lord Jesus Christ, truths revealed or taught by our Lord Jesus Christ.* These little exercises in which the children take an interest, are made more interesting still and permanently useful, if the children be interrogated on them.

Certain words used in religious language

have a meaning different from their usual signification, for instance the words *person, grace, species (eucharistic)*.

It is necessary to explain this to the children as also to make them distinguish the different sense in which the same word may be used, for instance *Church* (edifice or society) — *Communion* (eucharistic or of the saints) — *Contrition* (imperfect or perfect) — *Grace* (sanctifying or actual), etc.

We must avoid using very learned expressions when they can be replaced by others more familiar to our children; a word not understood is useless and repulsive. We should use difficult words only when they are necessary for the precise expression of the doctrine, or that they are in the catechism, as, *transubstantiation, communion of saints*.

When we explain words it is good to give *examples;* the best are those taken from things known to our children, in imitation of our Lord who always appropriated his language to his hearers. An intelligent catechist would not employ the same examples in a class where the children are employed at sewing and in one where they are employed in the garden.

We must endeavour to expose and *make known the christian doctrine* rather than give proofs of each point; that is the best way to protect the faith of our children. When, in after-life they hear the criticisms and railleries of the impious, they can say, the christian religion such as they depict it is not the one we learned [1].

Of course we should give some proofs of the truths of religion. For this purpose we should carefully present certain facts which may serve as proofs in such a manner that if ever religious truths were contested in presence of our children, they would not be shaken, remembering on what their belief is based. « Do not amuse yourselves by speaking of what may touch their hearts for a moment without leaving anything solid, but enlighten them by wise discourses and nourish

---

[1] « At the present day one is continually astonished at the religious ignorance reigning in the world... The most absurd ideas prevail regarding our dogmas and in perfect good faith people give the Church credit for absurdities which have nothing in common with our belief. How many persons in the world, very intelligent and well informed on other points, would be very embarrassed to answer the most elementary religious questions. — what is a Sacrament? — what is grace? what is original sin? and even who is Jesus Christ? what is the Incarnation? what is the Redemption? » (Mgr Dupanloup.)

their minds by wise instructions. » (*Inst.*, ch. II.)

We should not stop to develop the objections of the impious, they would often be better understood and remembered than the answers.

In the matter of truths to be believed or virtues to be practised it is all important to distinguish between what is of obligation and what is not. We should not mix legends and pious beliefs, not taught by the Church, with the explanation of mysteries and sacraments. We have not the right to represent a thing, as the sentiment of the Church simply because it pleases us; we cannot even be sure that it would edify everyone. If we think well of ornamenting our lessons with explanations of this kind we should at least give warning that they are not articles of faith [1].

Neither must we, through false zeal or want

---

[1] « How often, » says Mgr Baunard, « have I heard pious persons insist before men, upright although not christian and who undoubtedly would have become such if they had only to believe our mysteries but who could not bear to hear themselves called infidels because they hesitated to believe certain legends, certain visions, certain miracles, not of faith, which were placed on the same line as the Gospel. »

of light, represent as sin and above all as mortal sin, what is not forbidden or is only venial. We would be the cause of our children sinning even mortally, through false conscience, where there is only imperfection or venial sin.

Let us not venture too far in defining what is venial or mortal sin. The best directors of conscience are often embarrassed to decide such cases. Particularly in what regards modesty let us not pronounce; we should inspire horror of all that can wound it in any way without specifying the gravity of the fault [1].

Our children, on leaving the Good Shepherd should have, as far as it depends on us, an exact and complete knowledge of the principal points of religion. We would expose ourselves to the risk of not obtaining this end if, in our explanations, we stopped too long

---

[1] Let us remember on this subject the words of our holy Constitutions : « The Sisters who are appointed to instruct these same penitents, shall be very circumspect on this point, and take great care never to speak directly or indirectly, of the sin contrary to this virtue ; it will be sufficient that they inspire them with a horror of sin in general, and point out to them the misery of a soul at enmity with God, and who is the object of his wrath. »

at points of detail and unnecessary questions.

We should not fear *to return often to the same truths*. All persons who have taught them, know only too well how often the same thing must be repeated before it is engraven on the mind. Our children do not always listen, they are sometimes disturbed, the work they do during the catechism divides their attention; even when we come back often to the same question it is not sure that it has been heard, and much less, understood and remembered, by all.

Many amongst them have never received religious instruction, or have neglected the means of retaining what they learned; the words of the catechism are for them the words of an unknown language; they paint in their minds things entirely new and above their comprehension. We must not expect that a child will accustom herself all at once to these words and these things.

A good means to aid our children to remember our instructions, is to make them remark that such or such a mystery or truth is expressed in the prayers they recite every day. In this way we would enable them to understand the prayers and recite them with more attention.

A Mistress should be sure that the children have understood and remembered what she has said; if not, she should repeat her explanations, otherwise her instructions will not make a lasting impression.

Neither would she attain the desired end, if she always questioned the same children, especially if she foresaw that they would give satisfactory answers. Without neglecting the more attentive and intelligent children, she should rather question those who have more difficulty to understand or who are more tempted not to listen.

As to children incapable of learning or of answering properly it is better to avoid questioning them in public; we would only lose our time in a manner humiliating and painful for them and tiresome for the others. We should take these children apart and « have patience to make them understand and remember the things as well as they can, bringing them to the level of their comprehension ». (*Inst.*, ch. L)

The new children and those who are to remain but a short time in the house ought also to be the object of our particular attention.

If the Mistresses cannot themselves take care of the less instructed children, let them confide them to other children of whose religious knowledge, virtue, and devotedness, they are assured.

If a child be appointed to hear her companions recite the catechism, the Mistress charged with the surveillance during that time will do all in her power to have the duty as well done as if she herself fulfilled the function.

To teach the catechism properly, it is necessary to prepare it, by reading attentively the lesson to be explained and foreseeing the explanations to be given [1]. It would be well to take these measures several days beforehand, if possible, so that if we meet with difficulties we might seek an explanation from some sister or from the Reverend Chaplain or in a book.

As regards the care and dispositions necessary for this preparation let us listen to the words of our Venerable Mother Foundress :

---

[1] It would be useful to write some notes on the margin of the catechism. This precaution would help to remind us of what we intended to say, and spare us the trouble of preparation at a future time. For these notes we might use inter-folios that is to say blank leaves between the printed ones; it is easy to have books bound in this way.

« Let your instructions to the penitents be delivered with charity and great kindness; let them be persuaded that your whole care is to procure their welfare, let all that you say convey some lesson. For example, when you speak to them of the light of the Gospel which has spread throughout the world, make them consider how this same light has enlightened them and led them to the house of the Lord. Support what you say by sentences from Holy Scripture, then in concluding relate some edifying story. If your instruction be on penance you can appropriately speak to them of the ancient anchorites.

« The poor children take great pleasure in these instructions, brought within their comprehension by examples. How often I have most successfully used this means to keep them good and quiet! The simple promise of one of these instructions was sufficient to keep them orderly and good for several days.

« Poor children! beaten about in the great tempest of the world, they have known nothing but suffering; they have never, at least some of them, experienced the sweetness and charms of virtue; it is for you to make them known to them. » (*Inst.*, ch. II.)

In order to prepare an instruction seriously we should foresee the stories we intend to relate to exemplify the doctrine.

And on this subject we must observe.

1. Never to invent stories nor put forward facts known to be false or improbable, such fabrications only cause religion to be turned into ridicule and draw on us the reproach of being too credulous.

2. To give the preference to the admirable and instructive events related in holy Scripture, both in the Old and New Testament. There we find a chain of circumstances prepared by God Himself who has guaranteed their trutht, that they may eternally serve for the edification of christian people. We must not on that account despise examples drawn from the Lives of the Saints, especially those that have been solidly proved. It is good to speak to the children, of the Saints most popular in their country and of those whose condition most resembled their own; they listen to and understand them best. We should give examples of virtues that may be imitated rather than of exceptional graces that are to be admired.

3. We should observe great reserve with regard to visions, ecstacies, or other facts,

even natural, which might excite raillery or mockery.

4. We should not speak to the children of extraordinary occurrences related in newspapers or religious periodicals, the divine or diabolical character of which has not yet been clearly established.

5. We should not be too lavish of anecdotes or spend too much time at them. The example intended to explain the truth should not cause it to be forgotten — to charm is only a means, not an end.

Pictures afford an easy and useful manner of teaching, but they should be well chosen.

We should prefer those representing the mysteries of the Life of our Lord and those which, by reminding us of the virtues and power of the Saints excite us to imitate and invoke them; in general these pictures are more profitable to children than fantastical ones some of which are so absurd that, with the affected words accompanying them, they expose to ridicule the truths of religion.

Teaching the catechism is a religious exercise; it ought to be performed with piety and sweetness. It would be sad indeed if we spoke of our holy mysteries coldly and dryly as of indifferent or tiresome things; our children would not be touched by what has so little effect on their teacher. On the contrary they would be greatly edified if they saw that we feel what we say; there is a wonderful effect in the tone of voice, the gesture, the attitude, and the look. What comes from the heart goes to the heart! All understand this teaching; a pious exterior renders those who witness it, pious, especially the little ones who naturally imitate what they see others do. The impression made on the young soul by the accent of piety is never forgotten.

We do not mean that it is necessary to have an affected manner, a sanctimonious tone and look. No, a hundred times no! We should never try to appear pious; if we be so it is well, if we be not we could never succeed in appearing to be so. « We should avoid affectation in our words; our language should be like pure water. » (*Inst.*, ch. XLII.)

CHAPTER V

Prayers and Devotions

Prayer is, so to say, the respiration of the christian heart; it is the condition and sign of the spiritual life as breathing is the sign of corporal life. When God wished to make known to the prophet Ananias that Paul was truly converted he only said these words: *He prays.*

The Religious of the Good Shepherd whose only ambition ought to be to bring souls to life, will have at heart all that regards prayer. She will neglect nothing that can cause it to be esteemed and loved, and she will form the children confided to her, to habits of devotion truly christian, that is to say, interior and enlightened.

In the first place we must be sure that all our children know the prayers that every christian ought to know, namely, *Our Father, Hail Mary, I believe in God, the Commandments of God and of the Church, the Acts of faith, hope, charity, adoration, and contrition.*

It would be well to explain from time to time these prayers and others usually said in the class, because children often say them without understanding them and substitute one word for another, thus completely changing their sense or taking away their signification. When that occurs can we say that they really pray when reciting these prayers?

We should take care that the prayers be properly said; that the children answer and do not change the words; that they pronounce without precipitation, without shouting, or taking a high fatiguing tone, and that they have a modest exterior. Nothing contributes more to devotion than to hear a prayer piously said.

Our children should not be over-laden with prayers and practices of devotion; that would tire them and instead of giving them a love of piety, might have quite a contrary effect. We ought not to judge their tastes by our own. The great point is, not to add new prayers — which might be only on the lips — but to see that each one acquits herself well and piously of the usual ones.

We ought not to prolong the morning and night prayers nor keep the children too long in the chapel after Mass; it is better to confine ourselves to those marked in the rule and *Coutumier*, observing a just measure in all things.

If we sometimes remark in the children a certain impulse of fervour we might add to the ordinary prayers some practices in accordance with their present dispositions, but that should be done only in a passing way a triduum or a novena.

If the ordinary prayers were too numerous we could not find place for extraordinary ones (triduum, novena, Month of Mary). We would be obliged to renounce these exercises although so excellent, or perform them during the time of Mass which ought to be employed as much as possible, in uniting ourselves with the holy Sacrifice, preparing for holy Communion making our thanksgiving or spiritual communions [1].

We should not judge the children severely

---

[1] A recent decree of the Roman court interdicts the singing or recitation in loud voice, in churches or public oratories, of other litanies than those of the holy name of Jesus, of the Blessed Virgin and of the Saints.

if sometimes they do not answer the prayers, particularly those said during work. Of course it is desirable that all should pray; by so doing they sanctify themselves and avoid vain and evil imaginations, but they are not obliged to pray so often; they may be absorbed by their work or, without being wanting in true devotion, they may fear the fatigue of answering in a loud voice. We may try to induce them to say these prayers but we must beware of giving them a false conscience by showing them sin where there is none.

We should do our best to have our children assist every day at holy Mass; if it be necessary that some should remain from it we should take care that it be not always the same.

We should know how our children assist at the holy sacrifice. To hear Mass well it is indeed sufficient to occupy oneself piously; however there are some methods more perfect than others. The best is to have the children follow the prayers of the Mass in union with the priest, but each person may take the method she finds easiest and most profitable.

It would be well that each child had a prayer book.

It should not be permitted to study a lesson of catechism during Mass.

We should have greatly at heart to have the High Mass, Vespers, and Benediction, sung very piously and as perfectly as possible.

When the children of the classes sing during the offices we ought to encourage them as much as possible, giving them time during the week to practise. Nothing attaches the children so much to the offices of the Church as participation in them. The more beautiful the chant is the more they esteem it and the greater also will be their love for God and religion.

But if we wish that our children have zeal for the chant of the Church we must ourselves show great affection for it and cause it to be loved, by executing it well. We should try to learn the best methods of plain chant and habituate ourselves to the simplicity of its melodies, very different, it is true, from ordinary music — soon we shall be surprised at the charm and power of its chords.

We must always submit with great docility to what is ordained by ecclesiastical authority — either of Rome or the Bishops — whatever consolation we might feel in doing otherwise.

Obedience to the decisions of the Church should take precedence of all else.

It is needless to say that we should inspire our children with a great devotion to *Mary* [1]. We will only remark that this devotion should be, as far as depends on us, supernatural, interior, efficacious, and not confined to sensibility or a love of flowers, singing, and pictures. We should endeavour to render the children's devotion constant and not the effect of a passing impulse, caprice, or sensible devotion. « The smallest thing suffices, provided it be constant » (St John Berchmans.)

It is right, in order to satisfy our own devotion and increase that of our children to celebrate with as much solennity as possible the feasts of the Blessed Virgin, her month, and even Saturdays, but we must observe degrees and not do always the same, confounding the greater feasts with the minor.

---

[1] « Oh! undoubtedly we cannot have too much devotion to the Blessed Virgin, we could never love her too much! Her assistance will never fail us and our Lord is infinitely pleased to receive our humble prayers when presented by the hands of our good Mother. » *(Inst.,* ch. xii.)

Particular care must be taken to have the beads recited piously. We should teach the children everything we think capable of maintaining their attention; for instance, proposing a particular grace we wish to obtain and recommending it in a manner to interest them.

We should always speak of the Saints with great respect and teach our children to honor and invoke particularly their patrons, the patrons of the class, the Saints most honored in their country, Saint Mary Magdalen, etc. [1]

When we find devotions established in our classes we should not disturb them to introduce others, although we may have excellent motives for doing so. In such cases we know what we are overthrowing but we do not know what we may be able to build, such reforms never fail to excite criticisms.

In order to preserve our children from superstitious devotions we should avoid propagating popular beliefs which *attach an*

---

[1] « Have great devotion to the image of the Saints; they excite us to invoke their protection, a thing most agreeable to God as He has been pleased to make known by numerous miracles. » *(Inst.*, ch. ix.)

infallible effect to a certain practice without being able to tell at what time or to whom this effect was promised.

It does not follow that we may not pray and have the children pray to some Saints in particular needs (St Anthony for example) or that we may not have the devotion to recite certain prayers, a certain number of times or during a certain number of days (novena or triduum) but we must put our confidence in the power and goodness of the Saints and not in a pretended certain efficacity of such or such a form of prayer recited a particular number of times on particular days or hours in a determined attitude.

It is not prudent to oppose devotions established in a class unless they be pure superstitions, or calculated to draw ridicule on religion. Nor should we think ourselves authorized to propagate a practice because it is in honor in a class or in a parish.

It may have been tolerated by wise persons who saw the inconvenience of opposing it, although of themselves they would not have spread or favoured it. If we be embarrassed how to act we should consult our Superiors or our Chaplains.

Whilst paying all due respect to local and

particular devotions we should attach ourselves especially to those truly catholic, that is, to devotions proposed by the Church herself, to those having for their object to honor our Lord in the Sacrament of His love, the Sacred Heart, the Blessed Virgin, St Joseph, the Angel Guardian, etc.

Our religion should be governed and enlightened by the traditions of the Church the teachings of the Sovereign Pontiff and the Bishops rather than by our personal sentiments, thus we will maintain everything in its proper place; the adorable person of our Lord before all, then the Mother of God, St Joseph [1] and the other Saints. We should avoid a manner of acting or speaking not clearly authorized by the Church, taking special care not to use in public new invocations or forms of prayer which might,

---

[1] You will then go often to pray before the religious monuments we have raised as signs of our gratitude for the innumerable benefits received from the Lord through the intercession of our true Superioress and Mother, Mary, and of St Joseph whom we have now elected first Superior and administrator of all the Congregation. You will never honor these sublime advocates as much as our Lord Himself honored and still honors them. (*Inst.*, ch. IX.)

unknown to us, contain sentiments different from or even contrary to true doctrine.

The best means of inculcating a devotion profoundly catholic is to make our children enter into the spirit of the different epochs of the christian year; Advent, the mysteries of the Holy Childhood, Lent, the Pascal time, Pentecost, the months of the Rosary and of the Dead.

« We desire that the Mistresses who teach the catechism should always announce the feasts and say a few words about each, in order to habituate their pupils to enter into the spirit of the Church. » (*Inst.*, ch. XI.)

We should not forget prayer for the dead; it is a devotion sure to succeed in our classes because of the sympathy of our young girls for relatives or companions they may have seen die. The thought of relieving those so dear to them will make them say their beads with more piety and even make them desire to increase the number of their communions. When we have masses offered for the souls in purgatory we might apply them to the souls of the children deceased or to deceased parents of our children who knowing this intention will thereby be excited to assist with more piety at the holy sacrifice.

Amongst the exercises of piety useful to our children are meditation, visits to the Blessed Sacrament, examen of conscience, and retreat of the month.

The greater number of our children are capable of making meditation; for some it may be a real necessity. When anyone has to be employed during the time devoted to it, at works incompatible with this exercise, it should be a child who has no inclination for it, or, if this cannot be, we should take care that it be not always the same child who is absent.

It is well to read, every evening, a *resumé* of the points which should be read in full the next morning; they should always be read so as to be heard by all and care should be taken that the book used be suitable to the position of our children and to the state of their souls in general, and such that they will listen to it with interest. The choice of a book is an important matter not only to insure the success of the meditation but also to induce the children to embrace this exercise willingly.

Leaflets giving an easy method of meditation may be distributed amongst the children.

We might authorize and encourage visits to the Blessed Sacrament, if our class be near the chapel and if it can be done without interfering with good order and surveillance; or we might erect an oratory near the class where the children could retire to pray. It would be well to place on the benches of the chapel or oratory some books of piety such as *Visits to the Blessed Sacrament or Visits to the Blessed Virgin*, by saint Liguori: our children would go oftener to the chapel if we procured them means of occupying themselves there.

As to the examen of conscience, we should stop during the night prayers to give each one the means and the idea of making it at least once a day; the children could also be instructed to profit of their visits to the Blessed Sacrament to make it more completely.

We might also afford our children the opportunity of making the monthly retreat and for this purpose two methods might be tried — the exercises made in common, all taking part in them, or each child making her retreat in particular, on a day chosen by herself. In the latter case we could have a list made of the names with the day specified for each. The two methods could even be used.

In a general way we ought to rejoice when we see our children apply themselves to exercises of piety, or any other good work such as charity, mortification, etc., spontaneously of their own accord without being constrained thereto by the rule. But it is more prudent not to speak of those we have remarked, lest we trouble their modesty or cause them to perform these exterior acts of virtue from a motive of vanity.

We must do all in our power to preserve the children from the habit of performing exterior acts of religion mechanically and without piety; and still more from doing them through purely human motives, which would give them only an appearance of virtue.

They must not be pious to gain our esteem or the esteem of their companions, nor even to prove their gratitude and repay us for our pains by giving us some consolation. At the very most could we appeal to such sentiments in the case of a child who does not pray at all. By tasting the things of God she may come to love them for themselves. It is clear we should never use such means to make a child approach the holy table.

To save their soul, merit heaven, expiate

their sins, and to please God and the Blessed Virgin or even the Saints, such are the motives we ought to accustom them to have in their actions, if we wish them to be truly virtuous. We should always inspire them with a great purity of intention.

CHAPTER VI

The Sacraments

It is impossible for a soul to make the least progress in virtue or even to form a good thought, without the grace of God, and as grace is generally distributed by the Sacraments, we should do all in our power to procure for our children every possible opportunity of receiving them. We should inspire them with great respect for these sources whence flow the precious blood of our Redeemer, and endeavour to make them understand the conditions necessary in order to receive them worthily and in a manner profitable to their souls.

The Mistresses charged with the religious instruction will then take care that the children be well grounded in all that regards the Sacraments, particularly those of Penance and the Eucharist. Our holy Constitutions emphasize this point in the Rule of the penitents. For this purpose it is necessary to explain in detail, twice or three times a year, for example, during Lent and at the approach of the retreat or of the exercises of the jubilee, the proper manner of confessing and receiving holy communion

I

Observations for the Confessions

The children should be taught how to examine their conscience, excite themselves to contrition, and present themselves at the holy tribunal to accuse themselves of their sins. They must, above all, be made to understand the absolute necessity of true contrition, and firm purpose of amendment which is an essential point; they must not imagine that it is sufficient to recite mechanically the formula of an act of contrition.

We should also dwell on the manner in which they should listen to the advice of the confessor, and remind them of the obligation of acquitting oneself of the sacramental penance.

At the time these explanations are given, it would be well to have read for the spiritual

THE SACRAMENTS

lecture, some work treating clearly of these matters.

Unless for serious reasons we should require each child to present herself every month at the confessional; without however obliging those whom we know to be badly disposed.

We should encourage the children to confess often and do our utmost to render this salutary exercise easy to them.

We should be careful not to prevent a child's approaching the holy tribunal on the day she ought; we might without knowing it, put an obstacle to her confession, by charging her, for example, with extra work which she would not dare to refuse. We should see that nothing occurs on confession day to trouble the order of going; we should not excuse ourselves easily by saying, that if the children do not go to-day they can go another day.

It may happen that a child ask, outside the confession day, to speak to the confessor; we should grant her request. This child may have committed a grave fault and we should not deprive her of the means of returning to the state of grace.

Some children have a repugnance to ask

to go to confession; if it happen that they present themselves at the confessional without our permission, we should not reproach them, but rather pretend to be ignorant of their having done so. Neither should we refuse the request of a child who might ask for another confessor than the ordinary, but we should take precautions to prevent the demand for an extraordinary, becoming a habit and degenerating into caprice.

We ought not to reproach a child nor even show astonishment because she confesses often. We do not know the needs of souls; there are persons, even virtuous persons, for whom frequent recurrence to the grace of the sacrament, is a necessity. We should not be too quick to tax with scrupulosity and self-seeking those who act so, nor appear surprised or scandalized. Neither should we reprimand those who make long confessions. It is a very difficult and delicate thing to conduct souls; we should dread injuring them.

In all that regards confession we should be extremely reserved in our judgments and still more in our words. We should never, unless for very grave and certain reasons, make in public, any remark which can directly attack a child relative to her confession. If any one deserves a reproach on that subject, we should make it in private, otherwise we might render confession odious.

We should never speak to the children of their confessions, nor allow them to speak of them. They might invent stories in direct opposition to the truth, if we encourage them, being sure they cannot be contradicted : malice or the desire to make themselves interesting often tempts them to this. Moreover, the respect due to the sacrament of penance, prohibits our trying to penetrate its secrets.

It would be a still greater disorder to allow the children to speak of their confessions amongst themselves. We should not fear to reprimand severely and even to punish those who hold such conversations.

In order that our children may dispose themselves well to receive the sacrament of Penance, we should teach them to prepare for it beforehand and not wait until the last moment. We might recommend them to prepare during Mass on the day they are to go to confession. We should also see that they have some moments of recollection before entering the confessional, and that they perform their penance on leaving it.

If it be not a religious who is charged with sending the children to confession and watching over them whilst they wait their turn, it should at least be a serious person, truly pious and discreet, and who has authority over her companions.

If we remark any disorder or abuse regarding the confessions we ought to inform the confessor, as also if the exterior conduct of certain children who confess often, were a cause of scandal.

In the same manner, if we know or suspect anything grave about anyone, particularly a child lately come to the class, we should mention it to the confessor; a bad confession may sometimes be avoided by questions he may put, when forewarned. However we should take care to give only as probable, facts about which we are not certain.

It is well to inform the Reverend Chaplains of the general dispositions of the class at certain times, or of the conduct of a child in particular; we need not wait until they question us. This recommendation has its importance; but the children should not know that we have spoken of them to their confessor.

II

Observations on the Communion

The Mistresses should explain the conditions necessary for receiving holy communion and of profiting of it.

We could not too often repeat that it is never permitted to go to holy communion after a grave sin, without having confessed it.

The most perfect contrition — even if we were certain of having it — would not suffice; there is an absolute commandment to make a good confession and receive absolution.

We could not inspire too much horror of a sacrilegious communion; yet we should not speak of it in such terms as to cast our children into despair, if they were one day guilty of it; nor should we say that those who commit this sacrilege, renew *the crime of Judas and will be punished as he was.*

We should make the children understand that a communion is not bad or sacrilegious unless the soul be in mortal sin. They often fear to go to holy communion after a contrariety or some other slight fault, particularly if it were public; they should not think, that in such a case, they cannot approach the Sacrament; such an error would expose them to the danger of omitting communions of which they have great need. It would be well to point out to the confessor the extreme delicacy of some, in this respect, and for our own part, avoid occasioning this exaggeration, by reproaches made on seeing the children go to holy communion after such faults.

We should not always oblige a child, before going to holy communion, to make reparation to a Mistress whom she has offended; to communicate, it is sufficient to go to confession, besides, it is rare that these faults are grevious. However we should make the children beg pardon when it is possible.

We should be equally careful not to fall into the opposite defect.

If a child told us on the eve or morning of communion, that she did not wish to approach the holy Table, we should not force her, lest by our insisting she should be induced to communicate when she had serious reasons for not doing so. It often happens that our children hide their real reasons for abstaining from holy communion behind some futile excuse; therefore we should not ask a child why she is not going to communion or why she did not go on such a day. In general, we should avoid, when speaking to a child, making allusion to her communions and should even discourage the practice of the children's informing us of their intention not to communicate; otherwise, they might be exposed to go to holy communion without the proper, or even necessary dispositions. In a word, we should not seem to notice those who communicate or those who do not. It would be imprudent to encourage a child who approaches the holy Table rarely, to do so more frequently — sometimes it might be desirable, sometimes not; however if we see a child endeavouring to correct herself, we need not fear to show her the advantages of frequent communion which imparts to the soul, strength to keep good resolutions.

We should bear in mind that the children need not have our permission to approach the holy Table, nor to be admitted to weekly or daily communion. The confessor is the judge in these matters; the laws of the Church forbid others to interfere between our Lord and souls.

If the exterior conduct of a child who communicates often, be really reprehensible, we can make it known to the confessor and leave the decision to him.

In some classes there are days fixed for the communions, for example, Tuesday and Thursday. This regulation has real advantages and is nowise to be condemned, but we must not oblige the children to choose these days constantly — they are free — they may have good reasons, which they are not obliged to explain to us, for preferring to communicate another day. Let us do all in our power to facilitate the communions of our children.

When we know that a child who communicates rarely, is disposed to do so, we should take every precaution to remove any occasion that might disturb her or make her miss communion.

A punishment usual in many classes, is, to make the children wear on Sundays and feast-days their every-day dress. This punishment should be used with a certain reserve, so as not to interfere with the communions. A child should not be obliged by this punishment to defer her communion.

If it happen that in the class in which we are employed, the children have the habit of communicating more frequently or more rarely than we would wish, we must remember, that the confessor alone has the right to regulate the number of communions. This is always a very embarrassing question : let us not meddle with it.

A single communion well made, produces more fruit than several made without due preparation and thanksgiving. We should then take care, when holy communion is given before mass, that those who are to receive it, go to the chapel in time to prepare, and remain there long enough to make their thanksgiving, as also, that no noise be made near the chapel during that time.

CHAPTER VII

Devotedness in our employments

It would be a fatal error for a Religious of the Good Shepherd to imagine that she labours for the salvation of souls, only when she instructs them, teaches them to pray, or prays herself for their intention. All that is done in our monasteries, refers, directly or indirectly, to the souls of our children. Rule, authority, surveillance, recompenses, punishments, work, plays, redoubled surveillance during the recreations — all is done with a view to prevent sin and increase virtue. What motive have we in devoting ourselves, to all that can contribute to the material prosperity of our houses, to all that can render our children happy during their stay with us, unless, the desire to receive and retain the greatest possible number of sheep in our folds? All our employments are established and confided to us to enable us to save souls. All that obedience demands, zeal also demands; whenever we are tempted to

DEVOTEDNESS IN OUR EMPLOYMENTS

relax in attention to our employment, we are by the same, tempted to relax in zeal.

Let us listen, on this important subject, to the words so strong, so persuasive, and above all, so authorized, of our Venerable Mother Foundress.

« We must set to work all our activity, without losing a single minute. » *(Inst.*, ch. XXVII.)

« I also recommend you to avoid running hither and thither, seeking to learn what is passing, and talking uselessly of what others are doing, thus losing your time, failing in your duties, and perhaps sinning against charity. May these words of St Paul never be applicable to you : « There are some among you who walk disorderly, working not at all, but enviously meddling. »

« When it is time for class, go directly, without turning to the right or the left; do not be like those who never reach the end they have in view, save by a circuitous route. » *(Inst.*, ch XXVI.)

« Redouble your vigilance. Watch them in the chapel, watch them at work; watch them particularly during the hours of recreation. In the dormitories, let a lamp, as the Book of customs prescribes, burn constantly during the night Let your surveillance extend to everything, without, however, annoying them; be like a mother whose eyes are fixed with constant solicitude on the children who are the object of her affection. *Let no misfortune, or offence against God, happen through your want of vigilance!!* » (*Inst.*, ch. L.)

« Another means of practising mortification, for those who are mistresses of classes, is to remain quietly in the midst of their flock, never leaving them under any pretext whatever. Believe me, the penitents will be restless when they see a religious continually going from one place to another; they then find it hard to remain quietly in one place, and when you urge them to be quiet and attentive to their work, if your words be not enforced by your example, they will be wholly ineffectual, and even irritate the penitents. The mistress, on the contrary, who patiently spends long hours in her class, who makes it evident that she willingly remains with her flock, wins their hearts, and succeeds in overcoming the most difficult characters. » (*Inst.*, ch. XLII.)

« You will sometimes find it hard to remain in class, in the midst of persons frequently difficult to govern; but, my children, bear in mind that the work of saving souls is a work of labour and sacrifice. It costs to gain souls, and usually it is only after much labour and long waiting that we see the fruit of our toil. » *(Inst.*, ch. XLIX.)

« You all, while you are in the Institute, labour for the salvation of souls; at least it is to this labor that your vocation calls you. Even those who are employed in the garden, those who are in the bakery, those who are charged with the linen, or with any office whatever, are all working for the salvation of souls. They practise the fourth vow as much as the superiors and the first mistresses of penitents. » *(Inst.*, ch. LII.)

« Had you no other occupation than dusting the stalls, sweeping the house, washing the dishes, it should be done with purity of intention and holy zeal. Be persuaded, moreover, that in a religious house, one who is faithful in the fulfilment of a humble office, often renders more service than another with a much higher order of mind; and rest assured that, if you are careful and faithful, there is no one among you that cannot be most useful in the office assigned her. Each member of the

Congregation should devote herself to the general good of the Institute. » *(Inst.,* ch. XXVI.)

« Our sisters engaged in the kitchen, in the bakery, in the garden, in the vestry, and in the linen room, work hard also; they should endeavour to do well all that they do, for they dwell like the others in the house of the Lord, where we must all with common accord contribute to the general good of the community. In like manner, those who are engaged in preparing work, must love their employment; they must not lose their time, but bear in mind that this time is not their own, and that, when they waste it, they violate their vow of poverty...

« Do you not give greater glory to God by working to support one or two extra penitents, than you would if, even under pretext of becoming more perfect you were to remain in choir half the day, or in your cell, occupied only with yourself?

« When you devote yourselves to the general good of the Congregation, you extend your zeal to the most distant countries; when you contribute to the support of the House where you are, you have the merit of all the good which this House does abroad. » *(Inst.,* ch. XLVII.)

« Moreover, my dear children, I wish that one thought should continually predominate in your minds; that is, that, as each of you individually, must continually contribute to the general good and glory of the Inttitute, so each one must endeavour to fulfil as perfectly as possible the special office assigned her. Remember, my dear children, that you are the instruments God has chosen to co-operate in the great work of the salvation of souls, that to you has been given the cultivation of the grain of mustard seed, destined to become a great tree in the field of the Church. To this end must all your efforts tend. It is for you to bring to the salutary shade of this tree the poor weary souls lost in the ways of sin, that they may be purified and strengthened. Now how, my dear children, can you most effectually do this? By the faithful fulfilment of your duties, whence will result all the beauty of God's house. » *(Inst.*, ch. XXXVII.)

CHAPTER VIII

The First Mistress

The Rules of our holy Institute, establish between the Community of Religious and the persons who are the object of our works, an absolute separation [1]. From this separation results the necessity of a particular organization which places at the head of each category, a religious delegated by the Superioress, to govern and direct it in her name.

The first Mistress exercises in her class an office analogous to that of the Superioress in the Community, but her action is always subject to the control of the latter to whom God has confided the charge of the Monastery. The office of first Mistress, particularly of the penitents, is very important; before confiding

---

[1] « Between the community and the classes there should be an immense distance because of the reserve Religious must observe. » *(Inst.*, ch. L.)

it to one of her Sisters, the Superioress should pray Jesus Good Shepherd to choose himself the shepherdess for His flock.

This religious should be solidly grounded in virtue, and profoundly attached to the works of her vocation; she should be animated by a great zeal for the salvation of souls, and apply herself more than others, to live by Faith, so that all her actions may be inspired by the compassionate charity of our Lord for the poor and for sinners.

She alone shall be charged with the direction of the class, the other Mistresses being subject to her authority in all that regards their employment. It is absolutely necessary that it be so. « There shall be in each class only one directress viz; the first Mistress. Not to hold to this point would be to lay the foundation of a thousand miseries, we earnestly recommend fidelity to it. » *(Words of our Venerable Mother Foundress.)*

It is the right that the Superioress see the penitents in private, once or twice a year, if she wish. The Mistress ought to facilitate these interviews, and have recourse to them herself when she finds her own influence insufficient over certain characters. But it would be an abuse if this intervention became frequent, and still more so, if the children themselves sought it, unknown to the Mistress; a wise and prudent Superioress will always know how to avoid such inconveniences. « The local Superioresses may indeed speak to the penitents in private, once in passing, but in general it is the Mistress who should remedy the miseries existing in her class; it is to her the *aides* should always send the children. »

This measure wisely observed will have a common advantage for the Superioress and the Mistress. The latter, in daily contact with the children, will sometimes meet insurmountable difficulties and be obliged to recur to the Superioress whose authority is greater because it is invoked but rarely, and only on grave occasions. If the Superioress were to punish the children, they would not respect her so much, and the influence of the Mistress would be lessened.

The Superioress and first Mistress bearing together the same responsibilities, ought to be very united, otherwise it would be impossible for either to realize the good to which she aspires; reciprocal confidence should reign. Happy the Superioress who can repose with security on the zeal and devotedness of the first Mistress! The latter ought to live in great dependence on her Superioress, acting only in the spirit of obedience, sacrificing, when necessary, her personal views [1].

She shall faithfully give her an account of all that takes place in the class, passing over in silence the little annoyances which she can easily remedy. She shall not be obliged, generally, to make known the intimate confidences she may have received from the children; if for any reason she finds it necessary to speak of them, the Superioress should prudently hide from the child concerned, cognizance of such secrets. It is most important that the children should be absolutely sure of the discretion of their Mistress; else they would not reveal to her things it is most important for her to know.

The first Mistress must watch over all and be, as it were, everywhere. She shall often

---

[1] « What ought the Mistresses of class to do when they are named? They ought to begin by placing their work in the Sacred Hearts of Jesus and Mary and resolve to recur often to them. They ought also to beg the Superioress to give them advice and inform them of her intentions. » *(Inst.*, ch. l.)

visit the different employments of the class, avoiding, as much as possible, having fixed days or hours for these visits. She shall know where everything is and keep herself informed of all that passes in the class.

She ought to be present when the children rise, and go to bed, as also at the recreation after breakfast (if there be one) and after supper. With regard to the meals, it is customary for the first Mistress to preside at the evening one; she should not absent herself unless for some extraordinary and unforeseen cause. She should conduct the children to Mass and assist at it while watching over them.

Nothing contributes so much to the maintenance of good order in a class as a little conference given every day by the first Mistress — it might be made at eleven oclock. This would be the moment to encourage the children who do well; remark the faults committed [1] and by wise and charitable counsels prevent those that might be committed.

When reprimanding she should not always

---

[1] It is better always to let the reproofs come from the first Mistress.

name the child in fault [1], unless in case of a public scandal; she should use the tact and prudence inspired by christian charity and maternal devotedness by which she should always be guided. Whatever be the faults, whatever the necessity for reprehending or even punishing, she should take care not to outstep the measure, and above all, not to wound the culprit by harsh words or reproaches *founded on what she knows of her past life* [2].

Even when necessity obliges her to use these means of repression, she should endeavour, notwithstanding the severity of her language and attitude, to be perfectly self-possessed, under the eye of God, and never to lose the calm becoming a religious. The least sign

---

[1] « When you perceive that a reprimand will only anger a child, speak in a general way against the fault in question, or address the reproof to another who knows how to receive it with docility. » *(Inst.,* ch. L.)

[2] « Even in private conversations, such allusions are to be avoided. There would be great danger in speaking to penitents of their past faults. It would scandalize them very much if you touched ever so lightly on certain matters; for they are persuaded that religious are far from conceiving any thought of such things. » *(Inst.,* ch. LII.)

of hastiness, would only diminish her authority and lessen the effect of her just observations. We should condemn evil as it merits, at the same time being careful not to scandalize by our irritation [1].

The reprimand once given she should never revert to the fault which has merited it, nor make any allusion to it, but rather pretend to have forgotten it. If she fail in this rule she will only embitter the children without doing any good. Let her remember the divine mercy; when God has pardoned a sinner, He forgets the sin and has only tenderness and compassion for the culprit.

Every week, the Mistress will give a particular instruction on a truth of faith, on

---

[1] « To bring them back to God, it is better generally to speak little and punish rarely. A life of prayer is more effective, in correcting them, than a thousand fine counsels. Piety speaks to their hearts more than the most beautiful discourses, and piety, above all, is what you must inspire in them.

« You must win them by manners wholly contrary to those to which they are accustomed. Treat the rudest with the greatest delicacy, speak to them in the gentlest terms, and spare them everything that would excite them to impatience, or would dishearten them. » *(Inst., ch. LII.)*

the Sacraments, or the feats of the Church [1], exciting the children to piety; teaching them to prepare well for the reception of the Sacraments of Penance and the holy Eucharist; and pointing out the means of celebrating the feasts with devotion. She might also explain the more important questions of the catechism, unless a Mistress has been especially appointed by the Superioress, to give religious instruction.

She will often recommend fidelity to the regulations of the class, and respect for established customs; in a word she will make these little conferences a powerful means of maintaining piety, good order, and a good spirit in the class. She may be persuaded that this exercise renders the accomplishment of duty easier for the children, and simplifies the difficulties and responsibilities of her charge.

She should never weary of renewing the same recommendations and the same advices,

---

[1] We desire particularly that the Mistresses who teach catechism, should never fail to announce the feasts and to say a few words in explanation of them, in order to accustom the hearts they are forming, to enter into the spirit of the Church. » *(Inst.,* ch. II.)

remembering that a good Mistress should prevent faults, in order to punish rarely. Reiterated warnings keep the children on their guard to avoid infractions.

Once a week she will assemble her *aides*, to learn from them what has transpired, and to give them her orders. On such occasions she will instruct them in their duty as Mistresses and make the recommendations she thinks necessary regarding the class. She must not communicate to them what the penitents have confided to her on the subject of their past life.

The first Mistress shall endeavour to maintain concord between her Sisters and the children; the first condition to obtain this result, is, that all be done in order, that everyone be at her post and acquit herself exactly of her charge, and that no one interfere in any other functions than those assigned her.

The first Mistress will herself give the example of regularity in the exact accomplishment of all her duties; her regularity will be a powerful stimulant for her sisters. She should have herself replaced in the class, when it is necessary to conduct the children to the parlor. It is important that she accompany there, children who are difficult or inclined to complain. It is also well to go with those who are good and satisfactory; the parents are thereby flattered and the children encouraged.

« In the parlor, observe consummate wisdom and prudence, endeavour to bear yourselves with the noble dignity and courteous affability becoming a religious. Avoid anything in your conversation which savours of pride or rudeness, which would suffice to give much disedification, excite in the evil disposed still greater hatred against religious Orders, and give rise to innumerable reports against us.

« Go promptly to the parlor when you are summoned, that you may not excite the impatience of visitors, or prejudice them against us. Sometimes a poor workman deprives himself of his dinner, to come to see his daughter, if you keep him waiting, he may lose the forty cents he has gained, and then who will give supper to his little ones in the evening? We must be kind, extremely kind, to working men.

« We also recommend you never to speak in the parlor of what goes on in the house, unless it is something edifying, likely to interest outsiders, and contribute to the good of the establishment. » *(Inst.,* ch. xli.)

We could never be too discreet on this point.

As the greater number of our children are not called to remain all their life in the cloister, they should be formed so as to be able, on leaving the Good Shepherd, to earn an honest livelihood and one day take their place at the head of a family [1]. They should be taught housework; some time of each month should be employed teaching them to mend their clothes, and every means taken to train them to habits of order and cleanliness.

The time for recreation is determined by the Rule. The Mistress should watch that it be not prolonged beyond the hour fixed. On days

---

[1] « It is very important that the preservation children and orphans, be well instructed in reading, writing, arithmetic, etc. If they be educated and know how to work, the young girls will not only be able to support themselves, but also their parents. Teach them to show great respect to their parents, and great devotion to their families. » *(Inst.,* ch. l.)

of great rejoicing, different pastimes and promenades should beguile the time, otherwise these recreations may become occasions of sin and draw down the wrath of God on a class. The recreations are in truth the most dangerous moments for the children's souls.

The first Mistress should, if she possibly can, undertake herself some hours of surveillance in the class. Her presence in the midst of the children will be for them an encouragement and a consolation and will moreover maintain good order. « She should be delighted to be in the midst of her children; nothing is more beneficial in an establishment, than the faithful presence of the first Mistress; she should remember that she is charged not only with the minutest details, but that she is obliged to to watch over souls for whom she will have to render an account. » (*Inst.*, ch. L.)

She ought also to arrange a time at which she may see in private any child who wishes to speak thus, or others who may require reprimanding or encouragement. She will show in these cases, the most compassionate charity, remembering that she has received from the Good Shepherd the delicate mission of bandaging the wounds of erring sheep brought back by Him to the fold kept by her in His name. « You must serve both as guides and mothers to the children of the classes; they should find in you comfort in their trials and help in their troubles. The greater the spiritual maladies of our penitents, the greater should be our interest in them. The more inclined they are to evil, the greater should be our compassion for them [1] » *(Inst.,* ch. XLIX.)

The first Mistress will find in the children of Mary and the Consecrated, precious auxiliaries, but she must guard against being influenced by the communications she receives from them. She may receive them kindly, testify her confidence in them, listen to them with attention, whilst reserving to herself the right of examining the facts with prudence. She shall not act, if there be reason to do so, until she has assured herself of the exactitude of their statements and has weighed the matter before God, asking him for grace and light to decide the course which shall redound most to his glory and the good of souls.

---

[1] These words addressed to all our sisters apply specially to the first Mistress in her particular dealings with the children..

A card indicating the hours and days at which visits are allowed, should be hung in the exterior parlour. This regulation should be enforced, at least with regard to persons living in the town. Of course we could not send away those who come from a distance.

The mistress must watch carefully over the correspondence. Though she may not be able to read all the letters herself, she must, nevertheless, know their contents, from the person delegated by her to read them, and she shall withhold any letter she believes would be detrimental to the child to whom it is addressed; a journal or newspaper of any kind must never reach the children. If the Mistress hear any news which would pain the children and which she is certain will reach them sooner or later, she should break it to them herself, suppressing, as far as possible, doleful details.

When speaking to the Sisters in presence of the children, the first mistress will guard against manifesting towards them the slightest displeasure (except under very exceptional circumstances) or reproach, on the contrary, she will treat them in such a manner, as to edify and impress the children.

To draw God's blessing on herself and the souls confided to her, the first Mistress will herself practise particular devotions, endeavouring to gain many friends amongst the saints in heaven. She should be specially devoted to the souls in purgatory, assuring to herself their protection, by having some masses said for their intention. While honoring the Angel Guardians she will beg them to watch over her, and for her where her vigilance does not extend to.

Finally, to inspire piety in children who have none and augment it in those who already have some, she will most carefully choose the lecture books. If possible, that for the two oclock lecture, should treat of feasts and the different times of the ecclesiastical year, or it might have reference to the needs of the souls of whom she has charge; in a word the lectures should be instructive and at the same time nourish and fortify piety.

In the refectory less serious matter should be read, for example, well-chosen lives of the Saints or other interesting works, on a par with the children's comprehension and from which profit may be drawn.

There might also be read once a day something amusing or distracting; the mistress must see in advance that such reading does not treat of morals, nor make mention of suicide, revolt, or affections too tender [1].

The first Mistress ought to give reasonably and charitably all that is necessary for the different employments of the class and for each child in particular. In order to be faithful to her vow of poverty she should take the precaution of asking all necessary permissions, never forgetting that she is a Religious, and can neither buy, give, take, nor receive anything for herself personally; yet she can and ought to be large and generous with regard to the Sisters and still more so with regard to the children.

If she wish that the children employ their time well and apply themselves to their work faithfully, she must show a great interest in it, examining it herself when possible.

She will take care that nothing be wasted; that everything be turned to advantage. She could have fruit trees planted in the recreation

---

[1] « Read no books of piety that are not approved, and do not permit the penitents to read amusing tales and books of which you are ignorant. » *(Inst.,* ch. II.)

ground and not allow the children to take the fruit, reserving it for certain occasions. Flowers should also be cultivated to deck the altars.

It is desirable that the different trades be exercised on a small scale in each class, in order that the children be comfortably provided for.

« Another thing you must assiduously cultivate is thoughtfulness. Forgetfulness in a mistress makes her a burden to her assistants and also to our children.

« Continually watch over and provide for their temporal needs. Before speaking to them of spiritual things, see that they have reason to be satisfied with the treatment they receive; do not imagine that allowing them to suffer helps to convert them. Treat them with nobility of soul.

« See that no one is ill without the Mistress knowing it; and when they are suffering, do not exact from them the same amount of work. Do everything you possibly can that the penitents may have nothing to complain of. » *(Inst.,* ch. LI.)

We might sometimes ask the children to do some extra work for a charitable purpose, such as to contribute to the *Propagation of the Faith*, to have Masses offered for the souls in purgatory, etc. We could prepare them for such little sacrifices by showing them the advantages they may derive from them, by relating some interesting facts concerning the good work in question ; we might also excite their ardor by procuring them some little treat.

The first Mistress ought to exact from the children an absolute obedience to all the Mistresses of the class and make them understand that the Religious charged with the surveillance, has the full responsibility of all, and the right to their entire submission.

The Sister at the head of an employment should have authority over the children who work there, otherwise dissensions would arise and the order of the class be disturbed. This right granted to each of her aides, diminshes in nowise the authority of the first Mistress but lessens the weight of her charge.

Although she should watch over the different employments and prevent the Sisters introducing customs unsuited to the class, the first Mistress should not suppress all initiative in her aides but rather leave them a certain latitude : some persons succeed better when acting in a personal manner.

The children should be taught to see God in all those who command them; thus they will obey more easily and their obedience will be more meritorious.

Not only should the first Mistress visit the employments, but she should assure herself that her recommendations are executed and everything done to procure the well-being of the children. She must remember that she is, so to say, the main-spring on whom all depends, consequently she must not seek her own ease or pleasure but be the first and last everywhere « the master's eye should see all ». However she should not go beyond her strength, that would be imprudence and not devotedness.

If every Religious of the Good Shepherd ought to be kind, the first Mistress is bound more than all others to be kind and affable; the rigor she is sometimes obliged to use should never stifle a virtue to which is attached the success of her ministry. She should be kind to her Sisters, kind to the children. If it be permitted to exceed on any point it is on this. It is rare that we regret proceedings inspired by kindness.

Charity should fill her heart to the absolute exclusion of all particular friendship, all preference for anyone; it should equally exclude all jealousy or susceptibility; even though it should seem inspired by love of her class [1].

Without being exigent as to the regard due to her she should govern with firmness and allow no one to supplant her. She alone has grace to conduct her class and she should always and everywhere maintain the authority conferred on her by obedience.

---

[1] « One of the things against which you must guard, is being so exclusively attached to your special employment that you are indifferent to the community in general and its various works. There may be those who are good directors of work, good sacristans, who are indifferent to the welfare of the community. It is well to love our work, the house in which we are placed, the office which is confided to us, but not at the expense of that spirit of charity and justice which binds us to every one of our Sisters, and to the entire Institute. » *(Inst.*, ch. XLII.)

CHAPTER IX

The Second Mistress and other Sisters employed in the class

The second Mistress and other Sisters appointed to aid the first Mistress ought to be very devoted and ever watchful to uphold her authority. They will cause her rights to be respected by the children and will themselves obey her in all that regards their employments. In her presence they will give no orders; in her absence they will have executed what she has commanded and will prevent what she has forbidden. According to the recommendation of our Venerable Mother Foundress they will be « angels of peace » between the children and the first Mistress, to whom they shall have recourse in all their difficulties.

« The aides should always send the children to the first Mistress. They should not say *Go to Mother Superior*, but, *Go to your Mistress, she has grace to advise you* ». (Words of our Venerable Mother Foundress.)

They will avoid all that could give reason to suppose that they are not sincerely in accord with her views and sentiments.

« They should avoid saying, for example, *If I were your first Mistress, I would do thus*. This language is disedifying to the children, makes them lose their respect for one who so expresses herself, and they regard her as not having a good spirit. » (*Inst.*, ch. L.)

The Mistresses ought to report to the first all that happens in her absence without warning the children of the account they have to render.

They should give neither permissions, recompenses, nor punishments, without her consent. Still less should they undertake to direct the children, or receive any confidences from them, particularly regarding their conduct in the world [1].

---

[1] « If you are not the first Mistress, never suffer one of our dear penitents to give you the slightest confidence.

« Penitents find innumerable pretexts for confiding secrets to a Mistress, if they find that she likes to have them speak to her in confidence. There are some who would even be capable of inventing sins they did not commit and seeking advice under pretext of needing guidance. Tell them that such advice should be asked

They must however make the children obey them without having recourse to the first Mistress — her too frequent intervention would injure their authority. They may ask counsel when necessary and then give their orders with assurance [1], never allowing the children to decide.

If a child refused to obey the first Mistress, the second should endeavour to bring her to her duty, if she has been punished — to accomplish her penance immediately, repair her fault, and ask pardon. In case she resists, the under-Mistress should show displeasure and grant the delinquent no satisfaction until she return to better sentiments.

---

of the confessor, to whom they should make the state of their souls fully known, if they would receive, true consolation. You know our holy Institutions, my dear children, and you know what they recommend us on this point. Be faithful to them. »

[1] « It is necessary that the second Mistresses act with certain authority during the hours when they are in class. Nothing does more harm than this very marked difference between the mistresses when everything is referred to the first, as though the second were of no account. The first Mistress should manifest great confidence in her assistants; but the second should be full of delicacy and deference for the first, always predisposing the children in her favour. » *(Inst.*, ch. i.)

The children sometimes threaten to complain to the first Mistress; when we do our duty we have nothing to fear. On the other hand, when the Mistresses have to complain of the children, they should not be too severe and should carefully avoid embittering the first Mistress against the culprits.

All the Mistresses of the class should have but one object in view — to labour in concert with the first, to maintain order and make the children good christians, without ever stooping to considerations of personal interest such as to gain the affections of the children. The practice of christian and religious virtues, devotedness, kindness, and firmness, will assure them general esteem without their seeking it.

Perfect union should subsist between the Mistresses; if any difference of views or disagreement happen to arise, they should at all cost prevent its being perceived by the children. The Sisters should never speak of a fault that one amongst them has committed even if it were public, unless they could excuse it. When they speak to each other before the children they should be careful to say *Sister Mary of Saint Valentine*, for example, and not simply *Saint Valentine*, and oblige the children to speak respectfully. When they hear the children speak of the Mistresses whether well or ill they should be very circumspect; many motives, such as the desire to flatter or a feeling of discontent, may dictate exaggerations in one sense or another.

In almost every class there are children who exercise a certain influence over their companions; to try to destroy this influence would be useless, it is much better to win such children to our side and turn their power to good account; with their qualities they have defects but that is not a reason for not making use of what is good in them. The Mistresses should take care not to allow these children to gain an ascendancy over themselves, they must keep them in their place and govern them by kindness and firmness. The first Mistress may give them (if there be no fear of their abusing it) a certain authority, but on condition that it will be exercised only when neither she nor her aides are present. They should never be allowed to speak before a Mistress, either to exhort their companions to the accomplishment of the rule or to threaten to complain of their conduct to the first Mistress. If this measure were neglected these children would become troublesome and diminish the authority of the Religious, which should not be subordinate to that of a child.

At the Mother-House and in the Provincial Houses the novices are sent to the classes in order that they may be formed to our works and that their aptitudes may be seen. It is essential that the first Mistress make use of them and leave them liberty of action in the exercise of the employments confided to them, upholding them and seeing that they are respected.

We will close this chapter by an important recommendation of our Venerable Mother Foundress.

« We recommend you, my dear children, who are not employed in the classes, not to go to them without permission, and not to speak to the children when you have no charge of them; for, be sure that, when you are not named for a class, you have not the grace to do good in it, and you cannot treat with the children, that is, with the persons of our different establishments, without great prejudice to yourself. The children learn that in so doing you are committing an act of disobedience. A religious, on the contrary, who confines herself to her duty, who avoids observation as much as possible, who speaks only to those, to whom she is authorized to speak, commands respect, and if she is one day named as Mistress, she is highly esteemed and gladly received. » *(Inst.,* ch. L.)

CHAPTER X

Authority — the means of acquiring and preserving it.

The first and most indispensable condition of authority, is to be irreproachable in manner and conduct. To command others it is necessary to be master of self. One should never give an order when under the influence of any violent emotion [1].

We should never lose our calm, even when we feel that our endeavours to be useful to the children are repaid by indifference and ingratitude [2].

We sometimes think we have nothing to

---

[1] « Understand how necessary it is to watch over yourselves, that you may not yield to impatience. If you feel irritated or annoyed, you must refrain from giving a reproof. Fénelon says, that when one who has erred perceives that he who corrects him allows himself to be transported with passion, it is very difficult for the culprit to repress his. » *(Inst.,* ch. LII.)

[2] « We should, like the fig-tree, keep what is bitter for ourselves and give the sweet to others. » *(Inst,* ch. LII.)

reproach ourselves with on this point, and yet, the tone of voice, the expression of face, our angry look, show too clearly that we are wanting in self-control. In such a case we expose ourselves not only to lose authority and make ourselves ridiculous, but also to fail in that reserve which is the guardian of all religious virtues.

We should never forget the respect due to our children as souls made to the image of God, daughters of our heavenly Father, and members of our Lord. When we fail in respect to anyone, we are in fault, and thereby, less worthy of respect. At the present day in consequence of modern education, the children are sensitive to the slightest offence. — Our penitents are always morbidly sensitive. An offensive word may make a wound which kindness could not heal.

« Others again have a harsh, impatient manner of speaking, raise the voice in reproving, and are far from possessing that gentle suavity and dignity becoming a religious. They give the impression of being always in ill-humor; and yet many of them, withal, make little account of such faults, and hardly think of correcting them. » (*Inst.*, ch. XLI.)

We should scrupulously avoid the use of insulting, contemptuous, humiliating terms, or reproaching a child with defects she cannot correct, such as, want of intelligence or physical deformity; with still greater reason should we abstain from humiliating allusions to their family or other secret matters. Let us be grave without haughtiness, dignified without disdain. There are persons who exact much from the children but are far from treating them as they ought, such injustice should not be. Respect them and they will be respectful; by speaking politely to the children you will prevent their being rude.

« It is only possible to win them to God, by treating them with the utmost delicacy. In reproving them, never permit yourselves to use unseemly expressions, which will only irritate them. Yes, treat them with that distinguished politeness and courtesy becoming the spouses of Jesus Christ. » *(Inst.,* ch. xlix.)

We may be very sure that a modest demeanour will contribute much to gain the esteem and respect of the children. They usually judge us, with or without reason, by our exterior; if it breathe virtue, wisdom, gravity, self-possession, and kindness, they cannot refuse us the deference granted instinctively to moral superiority [1].

The perfect modesty becoming a Mistress, supposes a certain gravity.

« Avoid most carefully, my beloved children, those frivolous manners which take so much from the edification we owe our neighbour. » *(Inst.,* ch. XLII.)

In presence of the children we should not laugh loudly, nor cry, nor, except on very rare occasions, eat or drink.

A modest Religious speaks little. We lose authority by speaking too much with the children, because they soon read our soul with its defects [2], and besides, it places

---

[1] « To win souls to God, my dear children, you must be amiable. Endeavour then to become so. Let peace radiate from your countenance, and words of sweetness and gentleness flow from your lips, like a soothing balm to the souls of your hearers. Avoid any stiffness or coldness of manner; be easy, affable, obliging, and at the same time, grave. » *(Inst.,* ch. LI.)

[2] « I warn you to be on your guard against their wiles, to fear them, as you would the snares of the serpent. Remember, that while we are studying these poor children in order to know them, they are cunningly, I would almost say maliciously, studying us, and striving to know us. You may be sure, they examine you from head to foot; we are never free from their espionage. » *(Inst.,* ch. IV.)

us too much on a level with them. Even, giving orders or making recommendations, should be done in few words. An order once given, should not be repeated, and on no account should we enter into discussions with the children — by proving to them that we are in the right, we establish them judges of our conduct. The order is given, there is no need of explanations.

As irreproachable conduct is a necessary condition for authority we must be always just and equitable towards the children.

We should never give them cause to accuse us of unjust suspicions, infidelity to our promises, partiality, prejudices, exaggerated measures, or such things.

Mutual confidence and esteem are an element of union, as marked mistrust is a cause of disunion. The Mistresses will then show confidence and esteem towards the children, but let them not on that account relax vigilance. Young Mistresses must remember that there are cunning deceitful characters and that those who make the greatest show of virtue are sometimes those who should be most closely watched. Be particularly on your guard — this advice is above all for young religious — of those who flatter you; say to yourself — counting on my inexperience, they think to ensnare me and gain my confidence by fine words. Before forming an opinion of a child we should study her well without letting her perceive that we do so.

Firmness and kindness are necessary for the government of a class. We should never, under pretext of kindness, give way to demonstrations of tenderness or familiarity [1].

If a child show an excessive affection for a Mistress, the latter should assume an attitude of indifference, take no notice of the child, do nothing for her more than for the others, accept no mark of affection from her; she will thus rid herself of the importunity more effectually than by repulsing it openly, unless the child's manner be unbecomingly demonstrative. A natural affection, if

---

[1] « Love them most sincerely in God, avoiding all familiarity, all that is unseemly, and above all, particular friendship, otherwise you will be lost, and the penitents will have no respect for you. » (*Inst.*, ch. IV.)

« It would indicate that you still live a worldly life, if you were to prefer one employment to another, one house to another, one person to another. » *Inst.*, ch. XLIII.)

encouraged, may become as experience has proved, an obstacle to good, whilst an attachment founded on esteem assists powerfully the influence of the Mistress.

We must not confound firmness with severity. The former is always necessary; the latter rarely.

It is necessary that the younger and more difficult penitents fear the mistress; to them she will show herself a little severe rather than amiable, and although in general, frequent punishments are injurious to authority and order, yet, children who fall into faults for which they have been frequently pardoned, should be severely punished.

Firmness consists in a constant will which causes us to adhere to a decision once taken, without abandoning it either on account of the effort to be made or through affection or fear of such or such a person. Firmness must not degenerate into obstinacy, which would be the case were we to persist in exacting the fulfilment of an order, when new circumstances or remarks show its injustice or inconvenience.

Before giving an order we should examine if it can be executed and if its execution will cause no great inconvenience. It happens sometimes that under-Mistresses complain that their orders have not been upheld by the first-Mistress, but why have they given an order without consulting her or reflecting if she could sustain them?

We must never attempt to enforce obedience by showing anger; we are really strong when the children know we are firm and will not yield. Neither should we, under pretext of firmness, issue an order or inflict a punishment in a manner so imperious as to excite opposition. We should, on the contrary, act in such a way as to cause the children to accept willingly the determination we have taken.

When we perceive that a disorder comcommences to creep in, we should repress it immediately. Delay would only render reform more difficult, by allowing the evil to grow; and soon we would have to contend with a habit all the harder to root out that it seemed to have been established by the tacit approbation of authority.

A man of great experience [1] sums up in the following terms the rules developed in this

---

[1] Rollin, *Treatise on Studies*.

chapter : « Authority is a certain air, a certain ascendancy which commands respect and obedience. It is neither age, nor high stature, nor tone of voice, nor threats, that give this authority — but a character and mind equal, firm, always self-possessed, guided by reason and never acting by caprice or passion. These are the qualities and talents that keep all in order, establish exact discipline, cause rules to be observed, save reprimands and prevent almost all faults. »

CHAPTER XI

Observance of the Rule

The good order of the class and the happiness of the children require that the Rule be punctually observed.

In order to inspire respect for the Rule we may and ought to suggest to the children, christian motives for observing it; representing it as the expression of the will of God, as a means of pleasing him and advancing in virtue — by the practice of piety, fraternal charity, diligence, obedience, humility, mortification, etc. We must not however make them believe that the Rule, in all its prescriptions, obliges under pain of sin : exaggerating the gravity of faults, would give the children false consciences.

The best means of teaching the children respect for their Rule, is to practise our own most faithfully; in this as in all things, example is more powerful than words.

« A mistress who does not love obedience and regularity, may be certain she will never convert a penitent. » (*Inst.*, ch. IV.)

Consequently, each Mistress will be exact to fulfil her time of surveillance [1], coming always at the hour marked for her, keeping the silence exactly, and neglecting none of the obligations of her charge. A Sister who is indolent will inevitably be negligent in the discharge of her duties and we may be quite sure the children will not be slow to remark irregularities unnoticed by ourselves.

« Alas! if they perceive that a Religious has but little love for obedience, that she has a spirit of criticism, that she fulfils her charge unwillingly, that she is partial when she reproves them, they will say : « Physician, heal thyself. » *(Inst.*, ch. LII.)

Some persons when not in charge, do not perceive the inconvenience caused by little

---

[1] « It is further necessary that the Mistresses themselves be very exact in all points of the Rule, and that they have it observed punctually. Let each exercise be done at the hour assigned for it, not later. In an uncertainty the Mistress should say : « We will consult Mother. » She will thus win the esteem of the children, who will be led, by her example, to be submissive. » *(Inst.*, ch. LII.)

irregularities which disturb order and render surveillance difficult — such as, failing in silence, allowing the children to lose their time, speaking with too much indulgence of infractions committed, judging unfavourably measures adopted. This manner of acting, disastrous in its consequences — whether we consider general order or the good understanding between Mistresses — is always a sign of levity. It even betrays a certain preoccupation or desire, to be well seen, to be loved, to win popularity amongst the children. Needless to say, such conduct would indicate that it is not for God and souls we work, and would only draw discredit on us.

We should not forget that the rule is a means, not an end; consequently, if justice, charity, or any other serious motive, demanded a dispensation we should not fear to grant it. We should hold with energy to the observance of the rule but should not render it odious by excessive exigencies.

CHAPTER XII

Charity towards the children

Our children give every Religious of the Good Shepherd the title of Mother; our Congregation has the honor to bear the sublime name of *Our Lady of Charity*. These words are sufficient to show that kindness should guide all our actions.

Chosen as we are by our Lord Himself, to train to His love the children He has confided to us, we should respond to our vocation by great charity. If we do not by kindness gain an empire over hearts we cannot bring them to the feet of the Divine Master [1]. We should always bear in mind the recommendations of our Venerable Mother

---

[1] « A cup of sugared milk, given opportunely to one of our dear penitents, will be more effective in bringing her back to right sentiments, than acts of severity. » (*Inst.*, ch. LII.)

Foundress which breathe her affection for the dear children.

« You must serve both as guides and mothers to the children of the classes : they should find in you, comfort in their trials and help in their troubles. The greater the spiritual maladies of our penitents, the greater should be our interest in them. The more inclined they are to evil, the greater should be our compassion for them.

« Let us endeavour then, with gentleness and kindness, to sustain the bruised reed, and let us not extinguish the smoking flax. » (*Inst.*, ch. XLIX.)

« Ah! my dear children, we must have charity and compassion for these souls that the Church remits into our hands in the name of the Divine Pastor and their tender Mother, the Blessed Virgin. Love them; have great love for them. Console and strengthen the suffering sheep. Make them happy, very happy, with the grace of God; this is your duty. Do not forget that you will win hearts to our Lord only by charity. » (*Inst.*, ch. LIII.)

Our kindness should be drawn from the Sacred Hearts of Jesus and Mary; it must extend to all the children, even to those who seem to merit it least [1]; it must appear in all circumstances, even when we are obliged to use rigor.

Of course the Mistress will be kind to the children who are good and virtuous; they sometimes have more need than we imagine of help and encouragement; a sign of approbation is often the only recompense they ask. If we refuse this little stimulant, we may be the cause of a child's seeking in dissipation and vanity, the sensible satisfaction she sought in vain in the practice of virtue. It would be unjust and imprudent to expect our children to accomplish their duty as Religious should, without seeking any consolation.

A true Mother will show most kindness to those who need it most, for example — new children, the sick, those who try to correct their faults, those who appear troubled or sad. The eye of a Mother sees quickly when anything extraordinary occurs in the soul of

---

[1] « Love the penitents, whether you are directly or indirectly charged with them, love them with the boundless love of a tender mother; love them, whatever their faults of character, however unattractive their miseries make them. Love them most sincerely in God. » *(Inst.,* ch. LV.)

her children however numerous they be. An unusual taciturnity, less assiduity at work, less ardour in answering the prayers, a new companionship, sometimes a tone of voice, or a look, awaken her attention and excite her solicitude; not however to such an extent as to cause jealousy or favour a tendency to attract notice. Discretion is also necessary in order to comfort a child who is suffering, without letting her perceive that you have discovered the cause of her sorrow.

If a child has some family trouble the Mistress ought to sympathize with her and try to console her by increased kindness.

Each Sister ought to exercise attention and charity, so that the children may have nothing to suffer as regards food, clothing, etc. Here again let us listen to the tender words of our Venerable Mother Foundress. « We recommend you once for all, to be charitable to the children, to serve them comfortably, never to give them cold food, or leave them without a stove in winter. It is not just to choose the best vegetables for the Community and give the leavings to our dear penitents. »

Let kindness be the rule of our conduct, of our language, of our manner; thus the children may render testimony that we are, as we ought to be, true Mothers.

« See how the good God loves these dear souls. His miracles in the Institute seem to be done only in behalf of them. It is because of them, that we are wanted everywhere. Everywhere we are told, " Take care of these children. " We may say that we owe our vocation to the lost sheep; our Congregation would not exist but for them.

« May you understand more and more my dear children, the extent of your vocation in regard to these dear souls. I desire this above all things. .

« Love all your penitents, whatever their country. Devote yourselves to their happiness, with all possible zeal, and you will rejoice the Heart of Jesus, and the Heart of Mary. » (*Inst.*, ch. LIII.)

CHAPTER XIII

Justice

The Mistresses must always act in such a manner that they cannot be accused of injustice; it is a means of gaining the respect and confidence of the children [1]. They must be convinced that justice is a real duty, a sacred obligation from which nothing can dispense them.

I

Justice requires that each one receives her right.

Our children have sometimes the right to complain: we should listen to them without anger. It is well to know what they think, and it is better they complain to us than

---

[1] « You frequently ask me how I managed the penitents. It was by being just and kind to them. » *(Inst.*, ch. LII.)

amongst themselves. If their complaints be just, they ought to be taken into account. If the Sister to whom the complaint is made, cannot remedy the evil, she will inform the first Mistress [1] who will do what is necessary, without letting herself be influenced by reports made in anger.

Even complaints made calmly should be received with reserve, otherwise the Mistresses would expose themselves to fail in justice towards those against whom complaints are made. But it would be insulting and unjust, to openly show mistrust of a child who had never deceived us. In any case, we should be attentive and ascertain the truth, in order to repress the alleged disorder or to reprimand and punish those who merit it.

It would be tyrannical not to take into account, repugnances and physical dispositions, it is one thing to deal with little girls

---

[1] « Let us never think or say, that, having sinned much, they should be ready to endure everything without complaint. Ah ! my dear children, this is not the way our Lord teaches us by His example to treat sinners. » *(Inst.*, ch. XLIX.)

whom we may form to whatever habits we wish, and quite another, to treat with adults. Some persons, for example, have an insurmountable disgust for certain dishes; others cannot form themselves to a new method or a new kind of work; one may be an unskilful seamstress, but clever at other work. Let us remember certain sacrifices we were obliged to make on entering the novitiate, and that we should not exact as much from our children as from Religious. Let us treat others as we would wish to be treated ourselves. Some have defects they will never correct; we must bear with them without appearing to authorize them [1].

We have no right to impose on others, habits and manners not commanded by virtue or good order but only by an egotistical desire to find in others our own character and ways. For example, one who is silent cannot endure those who are noisy; another who is naturally gay has no patience

---

[1] « Be very compassionate for these poor souls; they have to do great violence to themselves, and they have many passions to wrest from their hearts. Do you think it is a little thing for them to obey, to keep silence, to work all day? » *(Inst.*, ch. LI.)

with those who are of a different disposition; one who cannot bear an open door or window cannot imagine that others are inconvenienced by having them closed, and so on. Our children have enough to suffer from the common and regulated life; if charity and justice require us to be tolerant amongst ourselves, they also require us to be so towards our children. This does not mean that a Mistress cannot establish new customs provided it be done with prudence and discretion.

It would be an injustice on the part of a Mistress, if, after having punished a fault, she continued to make life hard for the person who offended, or allowed the children to annoy her; such petty vengeance is unworthy of a Religious.

II

Justice exacts that recompenses and punishments, marks of confidence, public encouragements, and reproaches, be distributed according to merit and with a certain equality when the merit is equal. The desire to please or the fear of grieving should never make us depart from this rule. We know that we cannot succeed in pleasing everyone; we must be very mistrustful of the preference we feel for cértain children.

Justice does not forbid our showing, in private, more kindness or severity according to the respective needs of the children.

Even in public, we must not, under pretext of equality and justice, always use a uniform treatment, employing measures which as any prudent person could foresee, would lead to discouragement or revolt. We should take into account, age, character, services rendered, position acquired in the class, meritorious efforts, etc It would not be just to treat in the same manner, for the same fault, two children, one habitually regular and virtuous who had forgotten herself for a moment, the other usually insubordinate. In certain cases we might show more indulgence, in others, but less frequently, more severity towards her who is more virtuous or more prominent in the class; letting appear the reason for the difference. Without doubt, by acting always in the same manner and with absolute equality, abuses are avoided but certainly justice is not observed.

Merit and fault are not always where a first glance sees them — we should be slow in forming a judgment; slower still in expressing it publicly. In difficult circumstances, when we do not see clearly how to decide, we should be very self-possessed, never coming to a determination when we are not perfectly calm; this is an indispensable condition to our being just. We might fail in justice by acting when too strongly moved by satisfaction, as well as when under the influence of displeasure.

It is necessary to be very circumspect with regard to complaints coming from children of a jealous disposition; they are generally gloomy and dissatisfied, sometimes really malicious. If we act on their word alone, we may commit many injustices and cause much disorder and sin. A recompense given to a companion is enough to make a jealous child complain that, no matter how she acquits herself of her duty, she never receives any encouragement; if she be rewarded she finds that it is not sufficient, considering her merits; the punishments inflicted on her companions seem to her always lighter than those imposed on herself; if she see a child cared because of delicate health she thinks that in the same case no attention would be paid to her; if she fall sick she imagines that another in her place would be much better treated. She complains that she is set aside, when a service is asked of another, yet she finds that she is over-taxed and that the heaviest work falls to her. If, for peace' sake we say nothing to her, she is irritated and complains of being despised, and asks why she is treated differently from others. In a word, she would have the Mistresses grant all distinctions and preferences to her alone.

When we meet with one of these children whom we cannot satisfy, without being unjust, we should pay no attention to her discontent; but, act towards her with firmness, show her in private how unfounded are her complaints, and forbid her absolutely to make demands as contrary to justice as to charity. If we perceive that she makes efforts to correct herself we might grant her some little satisfaction even although she may not have quite merited it, in order to win her little by little to good.

CHAPTER XIV

Punishments and Rewards

As regards punishments and recompenses we must be extremely reserved. They are effective only in as much as they are surrounded by prestige, consequently, by granting them too freely, we diminish their value.

Before promising to give a reward or inflict a punishment we must consider, that, perhaps later on, a great number of children may merit them, and reflect, if, in that case, we could give them to all without inconvenience. By this means we will avoid the danger of not being able to keep our word. We should ask ourselves in time, if the reward or punishment in question is proportioned to the good or evil action it is intended for, if it is not too expensive or of a nature to trouble order or injure health, etc. We must foresee the circumstances — cold, heat, rain, the occurrence of a feast, etc., etc. — which might prevent the execution. No attention would be paid to our promises or threats if it often happened that they remained a dead letter.

It would be very wrong to yield to a disposition to weakness or severity, which would cause us to grant a reward or inflict a punishment, without being sure that the good work was really accomplished or the fault committed.

I

Punishments

Physicians distinguish two kinds of remedies, *curative*, which stop the progress of disease; *preventive*, which hinder its approach. The latter are certainly preferable to the former. Punishment is only a curative remedy and often a powerless one. The great point is not to punish but to foresee faults and prevent them, by surveillance — punishment should only be used as a last resource. « To succeed in leading the children to God, we should, in general, speak little and punish little. » *(Inst.*, ch. LII.) — « I repeat a thousand times, my dear daughters, you will obtain more by a wise condescension inspired by charity than by too great rigidity. » *(Inst.*, ch. LII.)

There are wild children who would not fear to buy, at any cost, the satisfaction of committing a fault, but if they perceive that they are always frustrated, they soon resign themselves to be quiet and make a virtue of necessity.

When we use severity it should always be unwillingly; we should never appear glad to inflict a punishment. Neither should we punish a whole class at a time [1]. A general punishment is odious because it often falls on the innocent, and risks exciting them to discontent and revolt — only the guilty should be made to suffer, but in some cases it is more prudent not to attack the most insolent because they would not yield, and, far from remedying the evil, we would only make it worse. By putting these aside, and chastising those who are more sensible to disgrace, we commit no injustice since the latter are also guilty; but it would be a shocking injustice to choose con-

---

[1] « We must also beware of punishing an entire class for the faults of a few : it might have very serious consequences. Poor children, who have worked all day, and who have made every effort to satisfy their mistresses, should not be treated like the disobedient ones. » *(Inst.*, ch. LII.)

tinually as expiatory victims, poor children incapable of resisting.

We should also avoid punishing too many children at once; otherwise, punishment instead of being humiliating, would become a cause of dissipation and amusement. Many faults and irregularities will occur in a class no matter what we do to prevent them : to attempt to punish for all, would only lead to fresh disorder. A prudent Mistress will shut her eyes on those which are the effect of giddiness rather than of malice.

We have the right to punish a fault without having specified in advance the punishment to be inflicted; but, when we announce a particular chastisement for a particular fault, we should explain clearly the conditions. If we speak vaguely the children will always have the right to pretend that they have not incurred the penance. The recompenses promised and the conditions for obtaining them should also be clearly pointed out.

When punishing, we should take into account the more or less deliberation manifested by the culprit, that is, whether the fault was plotted or premeditated, or simply the effect of giddiness. « When a child shows immediate and sincere repentance we may believe she failed through forgetfulness, and in that case, it is often better to pardon her or diminish the penalty. If, for some reason, we were obliged to inflict the full punishment we might make it less painful by a softening of voice and manner.

It must, however, be borne in mind, that some children, because of their very giddiness, do not correct themselves unless their attention is awakened by the fear of punishment; on the other hand, their companions take occasion to murmur, on seeing a pardon which they believe to be the effect of preference.

We should remember what has been said above : « When a child is badly disposed, it is, generally speaking, not the proper time to punish her. »

Needless to say, the penance should be proportioned to the gravity of the fault. Those which merit more severe chastisement are :

1. Faults against authority, such as, grave criticisms, insults offered to a Mistress, public resistance.

2. Faults against charity, violent disputes, humiliating reproaches, false reports.

3. Encouraging revolt or notable faults.

4. Faults against morals. In this case we

should be extremely careful not to injure the reputation of a child, or cause scandal by making public an act known to us alone.

5. Faults denoting impiety, profanations, blasphemies uttered in public.

The duty of inflicting the more severe penances, belongs to the first Mistress alone. Her aides having rendered her an exact account of the faults committed, should be satisfied with her decision.

The Religious of the Good Shepherd should never forget that it is forbidden to strike the children [1]; they should rarely give fatiguing penances, such as, holding the arms in form of a cross. They should never deprive them of food.

If we be obliged to separate a child from her companions we should never shut her up alone; solitude is a bad counsellor for a child who is not good. — *This point is of extreme*

---

[1] « We must repeat to you to-day, my dear children, a recommendation of great importance. That is, never to strike the children. I know well that none of you fail in this respect, but it is my duty to tell you to be always faithful to this recommendation. Ah! my dear children, never use harsh measures : they do not correct the penitents, and only render us culpable before God and man. Then let this prohibition be for all times and all places. Consider it inscribed everywhere, for I wish it observed everywhere, and on all occasions. » *(Inst.*, ch. L.)

importance; she should be given in charge to a person of confidence.

Long penances are usually unprofitable; if we sometimes impose them it would be better to profit of the first sign of goodwill on the part of the child, to remit the punishment in whole or in part, but this should not be done in such a way that culprits might hope to obtain pardon too easily. The abuse of penances, whether by prolonging them excessively or by imposing them too frequently, renders them ineffective. The children become accustomed to punishment, as the palate habituates itself to what at first caused a strong impression.

What touches a young girl who is punished, is, in general, not so much the privation of pleasure as the humiliation she feels. There are classes where the smallest penances have a great effect because the children have been taught to regard punishment as a great humiliation [1]. That salutary sentiment should be

---

[1] « A means which I found effective to make them understand, when they had done wrong, was to look at them severely, and, several afterwards told me that they would have preferred the greatest punishment to this look of disapproval. »

maintained: the penances should not be aggravated, but should always be regarded in a serious light. When punishment ceases to be a disgrace it ceases to be effective.

Exclusion from a sodality and privation of the badge should be the greatest of penances.

Three sorts of children require particular treatment as regards punishment.

1. Giddy children must be treated with severity, as it is the only means of making them reflect.

2. Thoughtful children are more touched by reasoning, and by being shown how blameable their fault is.

3. Bold, forward children, who do wrong expressly to attract notice, and even pretend to have committed a fault in order to have an opportunity of resisting if punished [1] — the best way to act towards such characters, is to remain calm and take the least possible notice of them, or, if it could be done, make what they intended to render themselves interesting, turn to their humiliation.

---

[1] « Sometimes their evil dispositions lead them to provoke us, just to be punished. This is the time not to appear to notice their faults. » *(Inst.,* ch. LII.)

II

Recompenses

A Mistress who makes a wise distribution of recompenses, being neither too lavish nor too sparing, will obtain order and peace and make herself loved by the children. Recompenses are more effective than punishments. Children who are insensible to the latter, are awakened by the desire of gaining a prize or the fear of losing it.

Recompenses not only stimulate by giving pleasure, but create a love of duty and authority. We should always show ourselves happy at having an occasion of bestowing them ; and regard the goodwill and application, rather than the cleverness of those to whom we grant them.

Recompenses vary according to seasons and places. Certain amusements which would be an impossibility in convents situated in cities, may easily be procured in those in the suburbs : a walk in the Garenne is a recompense much appreciated by the children of the Mother House ; in the foundations other pastimes must be resorted to. Each child has her own tastes according to her disposition, education, and early training. When we know what one and another prefer why not grant it to them as recompense, if we can? — It is evident that when the whole class is to be rewarded we cannot consult the taste of each one; we must choose what pleases the greater number, without regarding the preferences of a few.

A Mistress cannot too closely study the tastes of her class, in order to render recompenses agreeable. In this as in many other things, we must consider what is agreeable and useful to the children, rather than follow our own sentiment, as is explained in the chapter on *recreations*. Amongst rewards we may include good notes and points to which we may attribute a pecuniary value — a good note could be equivalent to a penny; a good mark, a half-penny. By this means the children can procure little extras for themselves, without being allowed the handling of money.

Badges of Sodalities are everywhere regarded as the greatest recompenses. They ought not to be granted too easily; the conditions on which they are obtained should be specified beforehand.

It is not necessary that the Sodalities count many members, but that those who compose them, be pious and conscientious; otherwise they would be a cause of trouble and scandal, rather than of edification. Every possible means must be employed to maintain the fervour of these sodalities, and thus they will be a powerful help to the Mistress in upholding order in the class. The children who compose them ought to be treated with confidence, but this confidence should not exempt them from surveillance. Whilst exacting from them more perfection than from the others we must not show them too much severity; if they commit a fault we ought not to reproach them in public with their distinction as member of such a sodality; it would be unjust to make their habitual goodwill a cause of more painful humiliations when they happen to forget themselves.

What we have said, applies particularly to the Consacrated. Before admitting them to take the habit, the Mistress should exact a long trial of piety, regularity, devotedness, submission, and good spirit. Once admitted she shall spare no pains to sustain their fervour and form them to the practice of virtue, frequently instructing them apart. She shall, as we have said, show them confidence, without neglecting to watch over their conduct. By showing regard for them she can make them powerful auxiliaries. When reprimanding them she shall be careful not to wound their feelings; she might turn them against her by humiliating reproaches made in public.

It is well to treat the Consecrated with a certain deference, but firmly and without shutting our eyes to their defects, and above all, without allowing them to domineer. They may be a great help but should not be permitted to govern the class. Kindness and prudence are most necessary here; the want of either would lead to most regrettable consequences.

CHAPTER XV

Work [1]

The Religious of the Good Shepherd, having in their classes, with but few exceptions, poor children who will have to gain their livelihood by honest labour, it is necessary that they form them to work, and inspire in them a love of industry.

---

[1] « Love work, my dear children : it is a means of preserving you from great temptations. Rather than do nothing, wind yarn.
« In our Congregation we must unite the office of Mary with that of Martha; let us, like Martha, know how to devote ourselves to exterior things, and, like Mary, keep ourselves in the presence of our divine Master.
« Beware of having any fear of work; remember that is the chief austerity which we practise in our Congregation.
« Great souls, prayerful souls, accomplish great works without allowing themselves to be disturbed or troubled... Never be indolent or slothful... Then avoid these faults above all things. Persons who do everything lightly, comfortably, without inconvenience, do not gain much for heaven.
« You should labor untiringly, according to your capa-

In this as in everything else example is more powerful than words. When with the children, the Sisters should always be usefully occupied, and if they be charged with an

---

city and the will of your superiors, never permitting yourselves to be discouraged, even by the thought of your weakness and the mediocrity of your talents, for, you must remember that all your strength comes from God.

« If you are ever in a house where work fails, then make little scapulars or embroider and knit, as they do at the Mother-House. But you must contrive to procure work for the classes; sewing generally suits them best. Do you know what pleases the Sovereign Pontiff in our Institute? This love of labor, this love of a laborious life; and to see that none of you fear the trials and fatigues which our works require.

« If we cannot do much, let us be satisfied with little, but let us never remain idle. Let us beware, above all things, of becoming useless to the community, through love of ourselves, through too much anxiety for our welfare, for our health.

« There are some persons always inclined to believe themselves ill; they have a thousand imaginary ailments, they exaggerate the slightest indisposition or discomfort, and give up to it to such an extent that they become almost useless in the community, as well as a burden to others, by their exactions.

« Even during recreation the Novices and Professed may sometimes do something useful, some may gather the vegetables, or prepare them; others may weed the garden, or sweep the walks, etc... All should endeavour to be in no way a burden. You will thus relieve your Sisters charged with the heavier labors, and they, full of gratitude, will send to heaven for their charitable

employment in the class, acquit themselves conscientiously of it. They should never complain of the fatigue caused by work, nor of the repugnances they may feel for it, nor consider a work beneath them, or not fit for their hands; they ought, on the contrary, to be ready to do all that offers.

The Religious who presides at the washing of a room, cleaning of a yard, or other such work, will not succeed in making the children work actively if she herself remain idle.

When sitting, the Sisters should not lean back indolently on their chair, stretch out their feet, place their elbows on the table, throne, or desk.

Sisters, the prayer of the comforted soul, so pleasing to God. Moreover, you can thus co-operate in maintaining a greater number of penitents, and then you also acquire experience in keeping a house, and you learn the rules of economy. I would like to have this system adopted in all our monasteries; besides promoting economy, it will be advantageous in a sanitary point of view, for nothing strengthens the constitution like exercise.

« Oh ! what a difference — observe it well — what a difference between the work we do, and that which is continually accomplished in the world, by the greater number of workmen and poor people !
. . . .
« If you were Trappists, Carmelites, or other religious, it would be different, but you are religious of our Lady of Charity of the Good Shepherd. » *(Inst.*, ch. XLVII.)

The Mistress should give her orders briefly and clearly, explaining distinctly the manner in which she wishes the work to be done, without giving her reasons : too many words only distract the children, and expose the Mistress to be misunderstood. She should not give too many orders at a time, but wait until a work is finished before commanding another. In general, orders should not be countermanded — once a work is begun it is better to have it finished, unless we see clearly that some grave inconvenience or loss would result. Frequent countermanding shows indecision of character, weakens authority, causes the children to murmur, to pay little attention to, and esteem less, our orders, and to make but little effort to execute them, counting on their being revoked.

When giving orders about work, it is well to specify the hour at which we wish it to be executed, so that it may not be set aside. The Mistress would do well to preside personally at important work, to assure its being well done; the necessity of scolding and punishing is often avoided in this way.

Needless to say, we should not command two things incompatible, or give orders contrary to those already given by another Mistress.

It is important that time be well employed; when a child or a class is unoccupied, it is to be feared God will be offended. We should therefore reflect and foresee what is to be done on such a week, such a day, such an hour, by the class or by certain children.

As to idlers, we must use every means to correct them — idleness is the mother of vice. We should try to discover a recompense or a punishment (the recompense is preferable) to stimulate them to work by hope or fear. It would not always be wise to expect to correct them at once; we should rather lead them by degrees to do as much work as their companions. We could call their piety to our aid (if they have any) and also inform the confessor of their defect.

Some children have a natural tendency to indolence, talkativeness, curiosity, or dreaminess, which paralyzes their energy without destroying their goodwill. They need to be constantly reminded of duty and encouraged to work; we might place them near charitable companions who would warn them, or we might do so ourselves by a look, and, when necessary, reprimand and punish them.

The necessity of employing the children and providing for their sustenance, ought not to cause us to overcharge them with work. « One recommendation, in conclusion, is, not to prolong vigils; not to sit up at night under pretext that the work is pressing. » (*Inst.*, ch. L.)

Some children have less strength or less capacity than others; it would be tyranny to exact of all the same amount of work, or punish those who are incapable of accomplishing as much as their companions. A judicious Mistress will try to find occupation for each child, suitable to her aptitude, thus the work will be done more satisfactorily, with less fatigue and expense, and at the same time the children will be happier and more attached to the house. But it would be a regrettable error, if a young girl destined to return to the world, were always occupied at the same work, particularly if it were of a kind not sufficiently remunerative to enable her to support herself honestly in the world. We should never lose sight of the end of our vocation as Religious of the Good Shepherd; we should in all things aim at forming our children with a view to their eternal salvation, and not shrink from the trouble of having them taught all that can help them in after-life.

The age of the children must be taken into account. The young children should not be kept sitting at needle-work; too much immobility would fatigue them and give them an aversion for sewing. Their work must be frequently interrupted by recreations or by some employment affording exercise; their hours of study should not be counted as *recreation*, since they are obliged to be quiet during that time, and movement is the principal necessity for their age. From a moral as well as sanitary point of view, movement is necessary for all, even for grown persons, but it is indispensable for young children; they should not be allowed to pass the recreation seated at their work. Experience has shown that nothing is gained by prolonging the time of work.

Children who give satisfaction and accomplish the task imposed on them, may be, with the authorization of the Superioress, allowed to work on their own account, in order that, on leaving the house, they may have some little resource for the future. The money thus earned may be marked down every three months and put aside to be given to them when leaving — the Mistress might encourage them by allowing a little interest on their savings. Some of this money can be given to them while in the class to procure what they require.

Some children apply themselves to accomplish their task, in order to learn to mend or do some other useful work; they ought to be encouraged by every means, by good notes or marks, according to their merit.

We cannot inspire our children with too much respect for Sunday. We need not be scrupulous — there are works permitted on Sunday, but it would be contrary to the spirit of the Church to leave for Sunday certain work which is done only once a week, such as general sweeping, etc. Our children should be so formed in our houses, that when they return to the world they will not leave their household work for Sunday.

CHAPTER XVI

Silence

We cannot expect our children to have the same religious respect for silence that we should have, yet it is a necessary condition for the surveillance and good order of a class; consequently, it must be respected, like all the other rules, with scrupulous care. Its observance will be, for the good, a means of advancing in virtue and true happiness; and for the others, a preventive against dissipation and dangerous conversations.

A new Mistress, on entering on her charge, should neglect nothing to insure the observance of silence from the very commencement; if the children perceive that she does not know how to have the silence kept, it will be difficult to establish it afterwards, even with the intervention of the Superioress.

The sign for the silence should be given the moment the time of recreation expires, calmly and without timidity, the Mistress should assume a serious look, show that she is decided and watchful, and from that moment avoid saying a single useless word. If any child continue to speak or go about after the signal has been given, the Mistress should look at her severely and not commence the *Veni Sancte* until perfect silence be established.

All the efforts of the Mistress to establish silence will be useless if she do not keep it faithfully herself, avoiding every useless word and noisy movement [1]. During the time of surveillance, she should not apply herself to work nor let herself be so far absorbed by pious reflections, as to prevent her observing what is passing in the class, but should watch over the children with a quiet decided look, showing a firm will and constant attention. If

---

[1] We should not only observe silence in words, we should also refrain from wandering or useless thoughts and avoid noise in opening and shutting the doors : « You will tell me, my dear children, that I never cease to speak to you of the necessity of silence. It is true, but our time is so precious, that, she who loses a moment in useless words, unconsciously does a great wrong to herself and others. » *(Inst.*, ch. xxvi.)

she relax on this point, it is almost certain that some disorder will occur.

Should anything reprehensible happen during the silence, it is, in general, better not to correct it then; if, for the sake of order, it were necessary to do so, it should be done briefly and with authority. If a child break the silence we should keep our eyes fixed on her in such a manner as to make her understand what we wish her to do — but, with bold forward children, it is useless to employ threatening looks — they would only laugh at them.

We should not give the children cause to believe, that when we see them speaking we suspect them of holding bad conversations; such suspicions are often unjust and it is always revolting to manifest them.

Some children have a mania for attracting attention, they are continually seeking to be noticed by the Mistress. The latter should not let herself be turned away by them, from the surveillance of the rest of the class. The best way to treat them is to watch those in their vicinity without seeming to see them. They would be glad to be scolded or punished, just to be remarkable.

It would be unjust to consider a child bad,

and treat her as such, simply because she breaks silence [1]; that fault may be the result of natural giddiness and exist in children really virtuous. A child who is endeavouring to be good, needs the esteem and affection of her Mistress to sustain her; if she feel herself depreciated she loses the confidence she should have in her Superiors, if too frequently punished she takes an aversion to her Mistresses and the house, and joins with those who have a bad spirit.

Another effect of severity is, that a child might form in herself a false conscience, habituate herself to the idea that she is bad, and by degrees, fall into grave faults. A child should be corrected of talkativeness by being deprived of favour until she amends, but it is always better to treat her with kindness than harshness.

If, during silence, anything occurred to cause the children to laugh, it would be an excess of severity to show displeasure, better let them enjoy it a moment, taking care however that

---

[1] « To keep silence they must do themselves unheard-of violence. » *(Inst.,* ch. xxviii.)

it be not prolonged; if we perceive that it was done with malice or on purpose to procure dissipation, we should immediately reprimand those who caused it; and afterwards inform the first Mistress.

The children should move about as little as possible during silence, the Mistresses themselves ought not to leave their place without reason; such disturbances always cause dissipation. For the same motive the Mistresses who are not occupied with the surveillance should not pass through the class.

In each class there are particular provocations to dissipation, such as, the actions of awkward or ridiculous children, noises from the street at certain hours or on certain days; accidents caused by the rain or wind, etc. These occasions should be foreseen, in order to be prevented if possible, and if not, to know how to act when they happen — whether to smile or look severe. As these accidents may occur sometimes with one Mistress, sometimes with another, and as it is regrettable that two Mistresses sometimes assume a different line of conduct in presence of the same event, it would be well to take the advice of the first Mistress, as to the manner of acting on such occasions.

When the signal is given for another exercise, the Mistress should immediately leave off her present work, rise, and by a look, direct the march, so that all may be done in silence and good order. It is particularly difficult to maintain silence when the children are being conducted from one place to another, and for this reason, there should be a Mistress at each extremity of the ranks; if there be only one Religious she should place a child worthy of confidence, at one end. In these movements the Mistresses should be all eyes, and very serious, to make the children understand that they must not speak. They should not have to wait because a door is locked or a Mistress late; if such take place, it will be difficult to prevent dissipation.

It is not by speaking that a Mistress imposes silence; an authoritative look, a dignified manner, a calm countenance, and self-possession, have more effect than the noisy movements and loud voice of a Mistress.

CHAPTER XVII

The Recreations [1]

The hours of recreation are those which require most watchfulness on the part of the Mistresses. It is generally during recreation that evil projects are formed, bad friendships commenced, that the children lead each other astray by conversations contrary to morals or against authority, by words equally fatal to those who pronounce them and those who hear them. Who can tell the ravages pro-

---

[1] « When you go to recreation go willingly and joyfully. Amuse yourselves in a joyous manner, remembering that the presiding angels assist in a special manner those who contribute to the entertainment of others. » *(Inst.*, ch. XXVI.)

« You must be convinced, my dear children, that it requires great tact to give them agreeable and opportune diversion. You will need more talent to make their recreations piously joyful than to give them beautiful instructions. » *(Inst.*, ch. LI.)

duced in souls, by bad conversations? The worst is, that these disorders are sometimes caused by those we watch least, because they have gained our confidence.

It is clear, that Mistresses who converse together during the recreation, regarding it as a time of relaxation for themselves, do not acquit themselves of the duty of surveillance. When several Sisters are at the recreation in a class they should be dispersed so that the children be, and feel that they are, watched. The right of granting permissions, should be reserved to one alone, thus unity of command will be preserved and disorder avoided. In the absence of the first and second Mistresses, the most ancient Sister shall exercise this charge unless another has been named to do so. The Mistress who grants the permissions should also give the signal for returning to the class.

Without appearing uneasy or suspicious the Mistresses should apply themselves conscientiously to know all that passes during the recreations — certain attitudes, the manner of laughing, looking, whispering, half hiding, etc., are bad signs and should awaken the attention of the Mistress. If there be well-grounded fears that all is not right, she should keep her eyes fixed on the children she suspects, until they change their conduct; but as we must always mistrust our impressions, it is better to say nothing, unless we have a positive indication of a fault.

When we do not understand what is said in conversation it is better not to judge ill of it. If a child happen to say an improper word, which she or those around her may not understand, it is wiser not to reprehend her hastily or in public; the correction would only draw attention to the word and and lead to sinful reflections. In this case as in many others we should turn aside the conversation.

The Mistresses should not let themselves be too much surrounded by the children during the recreation, nor their attention so captivated by a group, as to prevent their seeing the others. Children who seek each other, or keep apart, so that their conversation may not be overheard by their companions, should be closely watched; these children commit sin, rather than those who are noisy; the Sister charged with the surveillance should quietly endeavour to separate them and if she do not succeed, should inform the first Mistress. We should not, at recreation nor elsewhere, allow two children to be alone. If an exception be made to this rule it should be rarely, and only on occasions which justify it.

It is important that the children be all together in the place of recreation, where there should be no corners in which some could hide from the eyes of the Mistress. It is in such places the demon lies in wait for the children, to tempt them to do wrong. The Mistress should not fear the trouble of seeing that all doors by which children who wish to escape surveillance might pass, are locked; she should not allow anyone to stop in the class; on leaving the refectory, all should go at once to the recreation and commence play immediately. When in rainy weather in order to give the children exercise they are employed during recreation at some household work, they should be taken at once to the place where they are to be occupied. When the children are seated during recreation, each one should be obliged to remain in her place and turned towards the Mistress who should not tolerate whispering.

By organizing games[1] which procure movement and exercise, many sins are prevented, the children's health improved, and their sojourn in the house rendered agreeable. For this purpose we could utilize the gayer children who have aptitude for these amusements.

It is well, at least in classes of young children, to commence the recreation by some lively game, a round, for instance, which might last half an hour. A child should be

---

[1] « Have something pleasant and agreeable to tell them from time to time, to dispel their sadness and to cheer them. The Mistress who has the habit of remaining at her post without saying a word to the penitents will find it very difficult to make any impression upon their hearts when she wishes to give them instruction.

« It would be worse still if the recreations were sadder and more solemn than even the time of silence. You must divert them with innocent amusements. I would like you to have a fund of pleasant anecdotes to tell them; you would hardly believe how much such things please them, and help to banish the weariness, the struggles, and the temptations they endure.

« Remembering what I had heard a good Superior say of the danger of letting ennui enter the hearts of the pupils, I took every pains to preserve the hearts of our poor children from melancholy. When you see that they are sad, you must say a few cheerful words to them, induce them to sing a pious canticle, and use every means to bring them back to a holy joy. How many faults we may prevent in this way, particularly during recreation. » *(Inst.,* ch. i.i.)

charged to commence, all should sing and none talk; the Mistress taking due notice of what they sing, need not be too severe for the childish rhymes of a round, but as a general rule she could not be too particular about songs — they are even more dangerous than conversations. A song which does not appear bad often contains hidden malice, at least our children are capable of finding a bad meaning where we might see nothing wrong.

The Mistresses whilst doing all in their power to amuse the children should not make themselves their playmates, still less the object of their amusement; it is clear that by so doing they would diminish their authority. However, if a Sister happen to make a mistake that causes laughter she ought not to show anger, but rather laugh at it herself. In order to avoid being laughed at, the Sisters should apply themselves to correct their little natural defects of manner, speech, walk, etc.

The children of every class should be obliged to take their recreation gaily but with propriety and moderation. Screaming, shouting, loud laughter, rough plays, coarse language, and in short, every thing that savours of rudeness or vulgarity, should be severely suppressed. These recommendations apply to the penitents as well as to the children and are of great importance in a moral point of view.

On Sundays, the recreations are longer and consequently more dangerous [1]. When the children are tired of rounds and running, they should be occupied at interesting games such as Dominos, etc. This recommendation applies particularly to Sundays when on account of the weather, the children are obliged to remain in the class-room. The time could also be agreeably spent by telling interesting stories, putting questions on history and geography, or teaching new games. A good mark might be promised to the children who by these means amuse their companions, and also to those who draw most profit therefrom. By procuring scenes from Sacred His-

---

[1] « As for myself, I remember it was a great trial to me on feast days, when we could not have High Mass, and all the services were at eight O'clock. The Saturday before, I went over in my mind what I could do to make the new day pass pleasantly for our poor children. » *(Inst.*, ch. LI.)

tory, arranged as dramatic pieces, we attain the triple end of instructing, edifying, and recreating, but these representations should be short and well composed, otherwise they would weary the children rather than amuse them.

Certain days such as the feast of the Mistress, of the Patron of the class, New Year's Day..... should be marked by some particular feature — the entire or partial suspension of work, extraordinary amusements, etc. The Mistress should spare no effort to render these fêtes agreeable; they supply matter of conversation for weeks preceding and following them, thus much evil is prevented. Magic Lanterns and other such representations so easily procured at present have a great attraction for our children. Lotteries and fairs are also an excellent pastime for these days. Shops could be set up having at the head of each, a shop-keeper and cash-receiver. The Sister charged with the fair could prepare all that is to be sold, and draw up for each shop a list of what it contains, the prices, etc. — useful things could be sold at a low price, superfluities being raised, to compensate. On each list, after the name of the articles, some lines should be left blank whereon to inscribe the names of the purchasers and the sums received. The Sister guarantees in presence of the shop-keeper and cash-receiver the contents of the shop, before confiding it to them, and, after the fair, superintends the stock-taking. The money collected is given to the first Mistress who grants some rewards to the shop-keepers and cash-receivers.

CHAPTER XVIII

The Meals

It is necessary that our children should have good food, properly prepared and served [1]. Some Religious although good and kind, pay very little attention to what regards the refectory and kitchen. Being mortified themselves, they do not always remark the wants of others. Justice and prudence no less than charity, demand that we do all in our power to remove all subject of complaint and render happy our children [2].

---

[1] « We repeat again, my dear children, do not give to your children, cold or ill-prepared food. » *(Inst.*, ch. L.)

[2] « Carefully watch over and provide for their temporal needs. Before speaking to them of spiritual things, see that they have reason to be satisfied with the treatment they receive, do not imagine that allowing them to suffer, helps to convert them. Treat them with nobility of soul.

« Do everything you possibly can that the penitents may have nothing to complain of. Poor children, they

Many things may escape the knowledge of the Sister dépensière if they be not pointed out to her. The Sister who presides at the meals, should, therefore, keep her eyes open, and not fear to speak when anything is wanting; it is equally important that her observations be listened to, in such a manner, as not to discourage her from renewing them if she find it necessary.

It is well to know what the children say amongst themselves — some persons suffer rather than complain. Of course, they should not be encouraged to criticise, find fault, or be exigent, but, without questioning them we could learn their sentiments. They should feel that when a complaint is just, it will be favourably attended to; in such cases we should not answer them by exalting the advantages of mortification [1].

---

go to the refectory where they find a very frugal repast. It awakens in them a thousand memories; they think that in the world they could have whatever they pleased. They could go and come at pleasure : the more desirous they are to be converted the greater will be their temptations. » *(Inst.,* ch. li.)

[1] « Great tact and discernment are required, to speak opportunely : for example, the day when they have had a dinner which does not please them would not be an

When we discover anything defective we should not tranquillize ourselves by saying that it has always been so and can continue, that it would not be easy to do better, that things are the same in other houses, that there are many people worse of than our children, etc. We should always show good-will to improve, by consulting persons outside, learning how things are done elsewhere, etc.

We should never refuse to make an improvement, on the sole pretext that it is bad to change, that old customs are sacred. We should take into consideration the changes off the times, which have so great an influence on the temperament and habits of our children [1].

---

opportune time to speak to them of penance; on the contrary, say to them, Poor children, I am sorry you have had a poor dinner to-day. I am truly distressed. Then you will see, they will say : O Mother, it was nothing, it is alright. Another day you can speak to them in an instruction of the great evil of sin, and the suffering we shall have to endure in purgatory; and dwell upon how fortunate we are to be able to save ourselves from this suffering by practising mortification in this world. » *(Inst.*, ch. LI.)

[1] « Nevertheless, use discernment and be persuaded that in certain things, it is better to adapt yourselves to circumstances, doing the best you can, remembering

It is desirable that the Mistress could, from time to time, particularly on feast days, add some little extra to the ordinary fare; a little dessert gives pleasure to the children, encourages them to accomplish gaily an increase of work, to devote themselves in a moment of pressure, it is also a means of celebrating a feast more joyously, of recompensing sacrifices made to procure some advantage for the class.

I

Advice to the Sister who serves the children

The bread should be cut and placed in the serviettes, as near as possible to the hour of each meal, that it may not become hard; for the same reason, the window-shutters should

---

that, according to the spirit of our vocation, we should make ourselves " all things to all men ". In one of our houses at Rome they had preserved the French cooking and several customs contrary to Italian usages. What was the consequence? The penitents could not accustom themselves to it, they were dissatisfied, and it was very difficult to do them any good. In the other house I saw that the penitents were contented, fond of the religious, who therefore more easily won them to God. » *(Inst., ch. xxxi.)*

be closed or the blinds drawn in hot weather.

Fresh water should be put in the jugs, before each meal; when it is very cold a little clean warm water can be added, to prevent the children's health being injured.

The Sister should always have salt near her and if necessary, season the food which should be hot when served; and see that each child has what she requires. She should give a larger portion [1], to children who have a very good appetite, and the same to those who are employed at more fatiguing work; serving less abundantly those who eat less.

She ought to know the children who cannot eat certain dishes, and give them something else; but she should never inquire about their tastes nor encourage their caprices — that would lead to real abuses. We should be good Mothers but wise. The food should be substantial, we should have regard to the health of the children rather than to their

---

[1] « Use judgment, and do not divide among three, a portion of bread only sufficient for one;... and if you see a child whimsically refuse her portion, do not upbraid her with all her faults. » *(Inst.*, ch. L.)

taste or to economy. To those who are weak, the Mistress could give a little more meat, if it can be done without taking what is necessary from the others. What is left, can be distributed to those who desire it, but all should be done in silence; if it were necessary to speak it shonld be in a low voice. The serving should be done rapidly and cleanly, the Sister directing the children who aid her. If anything were wanting, it should be sought promptly; it would be unjust to give the children small portions in order to avoid the trouble of going to the kitchen.

It would be well if the children had little plates on which they could keep for another meal, the meat or other things they leave; but if they do not eat them next day, the Sister charged with the refectory should take them away — good order requires severity on this point — the Mistress should also see that if the children keep meat they do not eat it on days of abstinence. Everything used in the refectory should be kept very clean, the serviettes examined frequently, the tables wiped after each meal, and the refectory swept twice a day. When anything is wanting, the Sister refectorian should inform the first Mistress.

II

Advice to the Sister charged with the surveillance during the meals

The Sisters charged to preside at the meals, shall maintain silence as in the class, and cause all the recommendations of the first Mistress, to be observed.

Half an hour is allowed for dinner and the same for supper; at breakfast, the sign to rise is given, when all the children have finished. The children should not be allowed to eat too quickly; food taken in haste, injures the stomach. The Sister presiding, should moderate those who are too eager, and on the other hand take care that those who are slow do not deprive themselves of their food, in order to have finished with the others; all should be obliged to eat bread and to drink, during their meals.

The Mistress should also see that children who have remedies to take in the refectory, do not neglect them; some children leave them through forgetfulness, others because they are bitter or because they think them useless. If a child remain in the refectory after the others because she has not finished or for any other reason, she should not be left alone, a Sister, or a child in whom confidence can be placed, should remain with her.

After dinner and supper the children should be made to take a little exercise.

CHAPTER XIX

The Dormitory

Nowhere is surveillance more necessary than in the dormitory and nowhere perhaps is it more painful. There more than elsewhere our Lord requires of us a true spirit of immolation.

For many and grave reasons we should do all in our power to make the children go asleep promptly, and to prevent their being disturbed until the hour for rising. Nothing is so favourable to sleep as obscurity and silence. No doubt there should be a light in the dormitory, during the night, so that, should anything extraordinary occur, the surveillante may see it; but the light should not be so bright as to trouble the children's sleep.

The *great silence*, observed by the religious with a view to meditation, should be rigorously imposed on the children; the less dissipation there is at bedtime, the sooner the children will sleep. They should be obliged to go to the dormitory in silence and once they are in bed the Sisters or others who may still be up, should avoid all noise in their movements. The children should be taught to go to sleep with pious thoughts, and on awaking to offer their day to God. As much as possible the first Mistress should preside when the children rise, and go to bed.

She should be sure that the lamps in the corridors and on the stairs are lighted before the children commence to move, and should direct the line of march, placing her aides so that at every moment the greatest possible number of children may be seen. It is important that the corners and angles be well lighted, but we should not so concentrate our attention on certain points as to lose sight of others, some children always take advantage of the absence of the eye of authority. The signal to set out, should not be given until the ranks are formed, silence established, and the surveillantes at their posts; each child should be obliged to remain in her own place and to advance slowly. Order and silence would be more easily maintained by having but one rank and causing the children to recite a prayer aloud whilst walking.

They should enter the dormitory promptly, each child going straight to her bed [1] from which she should not stir without permission. When the children are in their places the surveillante makes the round to assure herself that no one is missing; then she locks the door and remains in the dormitory whilst they are undressing. On ordinary days this can be done in ten minutes, on Saturdays and the eves of feasts, twenty-five minutes may be allowed. The surveillante should stand in a place from which she can see all the children. When the signal to go to bed is given she again makes a round, stopping near those who are dilatory, in order to make them hurry; when all are in bed, a little prayer is said, and the surveillante retires to her cell. It is good however that she return to the dormitory sometimes and that the children know it, but she should walk very lightly; if she perceive that some of the children are restless she should try to find out the cause that it may be remedied, if possible.

---

[1] It would perhaps be preferable to have no curtains on the beds. Each child might be obliged to turn her face to the nearest wall, to avoid dissipation whilst dressing and undressing.

Before going to bed she locks the door of her cell and leaves the slide communicating with the dormitory open. She should be ready to interpose should anything extraordinary occur during the night : if she have not time to dress, she should at least put on her robe, guimpe, and veil.

The signal for rising ought to be given at a fixed hour; the Mistress should, if possible, be then in the dormitory. An offering of the day is made, all rise promptly, dress modestly and in silence, without anyone leaving the place assigned her. No child shall be permitted to leave the dormitory until all are ready (except those charged to open the windows, light the lamps, etc.) nor be allowed to work there. The surveillante should remain from the moment the signal to rise is given, until all the children have left.

If the children of any class do not rise as early as the Community, it would be mistaken devotion on the part of the Mistresses, to go to chapel, to make meditation, leaving the children without surveillance, on the supposition that they are asleep. The Sisters should make meditation in their cells.

When the sign to leave is given, the rank is formed in the middle of the dormitory, the first Mistress places herself at the head in order to arrive first in the class-room and see that all is done in perfect silence.

The surveillante assures herself that no one remains in the dormitory. Sometimes it may be necessary to leave a child in bed but *two* should never be, without surveillance; if a Sister could not remain she should choose as substitute, a child on whom she can rely: absolute silence must be exacted. When all have left, the door should be locked, and no child return during the day, without express permission.

In some countries a siesta is taken; it would be better if this custom were abolished.

Each dormitory should be under the surveillance of a Religious. The cell in which she sleeps should have several openings from which she can see all that passes. It would be well if it could be arranged so that the Mistress could see into the dormitory from her bed without the children being able to see into her cell.

The beds should be placed at a reasonable

distance from each other. Two children who have a tendency to seek each other's company, should, if possible, be placed in different dormitories, or at least, be well separated.

The Mistress would do well to change the children's places in the dormitory, from time to time; by this means necessary changes could be made without exciting suspicions or murmurs.

The closets should be placed so that the Mistress could see from her bed those who enter — only one child at a time. If the closets do not communicate with the dormitory, it shall never be permitted that two children be absent at the same time.

The Mistress charged with the dormitories shall be careful to have the windows open — in winter, when the day is at its warmest; in summer, when at its coolest. They should be closed before the children go up at night.

The surveillance of the dormitory is particularly painful in summer, because some children do not fall asleep as promptly as in winter, and others awake earlier. Order should be most stringently enforced; we should not fear to be too exigent on that point nor too severe in the repression of any faults that may be committed, but without showing that we suspect evil, or that we have any other object than to insure silence and recollection.

« Then redouble your vigilance... Watch them in the chapel; watch them at work : watch them particularly during the hours of recreation. In the dormitories, let a lamp, as the Book of Customs prescribes, burn constantly during the night. Let your surveillance extend to everything, without, however, annoying them; be like a Mother whose eyes are fixed with constant solicitude on the children who are the object of her affection. Let no misfortune, or offence against God, happen through your want of vigilance!!! » *(Inst.*, ch. L.)

CHAPTER XX

The Infirmary [1]

Of all employments, that of infirmarian requires most charity and devotedness. In time of sickness our children have a particular right to our affection, it is also the time they are most touched by it. A grateful remembrance of what was done for them in the infirmary will contribute more than anything else to attach them to their Mothers and give us influence and ascendancy over them. The prospect of being charitably and kindly

---

[1] « Never appoint as infirmarian in the establishments, a child of the preservation class, a penitent, or a Magdalen; they may serve as assistants, if you will, but they should always be under the surveillance of the infirmarian who should be a religious. If you do otherwise, and leave them to themselves, you may be the cause of their losing their souls; and, moreover, a slight mistake on their part, giving the medicine at the wrong time, or the wrong portion, might result in nothing less than the death of a patient. » *(Inst.,* ch. L.)

treated when ill, and of dying a holy happy death at the Good Shepherd, is a powerful attraction for our children particularly for those who are delicate.

The kindness a child receives in the infirmary may be the means of bringing her to God, or if she be already good, of renewing her ardor in virtue. Sickness by isolating and withdrawing her from her usual occupations, is a sort of retreat; grace awaits her in the infirmary, the infirmarian is its instrument, kindness its means of acting on souls. For the sick more than for all others we should be Mothers full of tenderness and devotedness. When a child complains of being ill we should listen to her charitably, examine her case and endeavour to procure her immediate relief [1].

In slight indispositions a little repose is sometimes sufficient. If we think medecine would do good we should hasten to give it and not send the child to her work until we are sure she is better or that the remedy applied has had the desired effect. Our children should always find us ready to afford

---

[1] « See that no one is sick without the Mistress knowing it; and when a child is ill, do not exact from her the same amount of work. » *(Inst.*, ch. LI.)

them all the relief in our power. If we cannot cure their sufferings we should at least compassionate them, give them hope that they will pass away and indicate the precautions to be taken in order to prevent their return.

We should not be too quick to send away children who come to the infirmary, because we consider they are lazy or too careful of themselves; before taxing a child with these defects we should have experienced her tendency to exaggerate and complain. If there are some who come too easily, there are others who must be sent and forced to remain in the infirmary. When we remark or learn from others that one of the latter is suffering, we should inquire into the cause and oblige her to take the remedies necessary.

An indisposition or accident, apparently of no consequence, might be serious for persons of delicate constitution or those predisposed to some disease. In the same way, what at one age is without gravity, at another, becomes serious. It is better to make the mistake of giving unnecessary care than of neglecting to relieve a real sufferer.

When we see that the remedies applied are insufficient, we should show the patient to the doctor, before the disease has advanced, minutely inform him of all that concerns her present state and the preceding symptoms; sometimes also of her former illnesses, of her temperament, and even of that of her parents. Details, seemingly insignificant, may be very important, consequently the infirmarian should say all she knows without waiting to be questioned, and even have prepared beforehand what she has to communicate. She should always be present at the consultation and ask how she is to act in case such or such an accident or complication occur before the doctor's next visit. She should be careful to remember all the recommendations and if she do not clearly understand some, should ask an explanation, though she should not trouble the doctor with too many words. It is needless to say that the prescriptions must be strictly followed [1]. We should add some little delicacies such as, biscuits, oranges, etc.; these little attentions give much pleasure to the chil-

---

[1] « It is absolutely necessary, as you see, that the Mistress be very watchful and the infirmarian still more so, and that those charged with the dispensary carefully explain how the remedies are to be taken. » (*Inst*, ch. L.)

dren. We should be very careful, in lingering illnesses, not to show any sign of being weary of nursing the patient, nor of repugnance for dressing sores. A sick child should never dread being a burden : to give her cause to do so, would be in direct opposition to the charity which should fill the heart of every Religious of the Good Shepherd — the sick draw the blessing of God on a house — we should be always ready to render them any service they require, and let them see that we do it willingly.

In maladies requiring services of a delicate nature we should let the sick person do all she can for herself. When it is necessary that she be assisted the infirmarian should charge a person of confidence to help her; if there be no one capable, the infirmarian will do this act of charity, with all the reserve and delicacy becoming a Religious, but without scruple. It is sometimes necessary to send a child to the hospital; in such cases we should be guided by the opinion of the doctor. When any child has to undergo a special examination by the doctor, the Mistress or infirmarian must be present, but through reserve, should stand a little aside.

Order should reign in the infirmary as well as in the class and dormitory. The silence need not be so strictly observed there as it is in the class; there should be a regulation on that point which should be adhered to.

Surveillance is more difficult in the infirmary than at the recreation where the Mistress who knows the children can oblige them to play, or separate those who inspire mistrust. In the infirmary, conversations cannot be forbidden nor can we prevent children of bad dispositions from being ill at the same time. The infirmarian must at least inquire what degree of confidence she may place in those confided to her, and endeavour to distract and amuse them when she fears they may hold dangerous conversations.

Noise should be absolutely forbidden in the infirmary; those who come there should be obliged to open and close the doors gently and avoid speaking or laughing loudly, for fear of fatiguing the sick who often, after a sleepless night, have great need to repose during the day. If care were not taken the infirmary could easily become a place of idleness and gossip. In the interest of the sick as well as for the sake of good order, no one should be allowed to enter the infirmary without necessity or special permission.

This rule should not be understood so as to deprive the sick of visits so necessary to cheer them — visiting the sick is one of the works of mercy to which our Lord has promised the Kingdom of Heaven — but we should prevent disorder and not allow the sick to be troubled by companions whose conversation might be injurious to them.

If several children sleep in the infirmary, the same vigilance should be exercised as in the dormitory. The infirmarian should see that they fulfil their religious duties; it would be well to have fixed hours for the morning and evening prayers and to perform some exercises during the day, such as, the rosary, lecture, etc., unless when the sick are too suffering : she should not leave the children alone, if she can possibly help it.

The sick require to be fortified by the reception of the Blessed Eucharist. The opportunity of receiving holy Communion often, is one of the most precious advantages of community life : our children should have the benefit of it. We should not fear a little trouble in order to procure them the happiness of communicating according to their needs and desires Sometimes the sick would not ask for holy Communion for fear of troubling the infirmarian. If necessary, the latter should miss Mass or Communion in order that a poor invalid may enjoy the happiness of receiving her Lord : that is the best act of charity she can perform.

The infirmarian should see that the children who are to communicate fasting, take, the night before, the nourishment necessary to enable them to wait until the hour of communion. To receive communion as viaticum the sick person should be in *probable* danger of death ; it is not necessary that the danger be actual and immediate. The infirmarian should therefore inquire of the doctor if a child is really *in danger*, and if so, inform the Reverend Chaplain.

It is not sufficient that a sick person be unable to remain fasting, in order to have the right to communicate as Viaticum. In some illnesses, patients are obliged to take food or remedies frequently and at short intervals, although they be not in danger of death — such persons are not entitled to communion as Viaticum.

Prayer and the pious reception of the sacraments are almost impossible when the faculties are benumbed by the sufferings which generally precede death; the infirmarian should then not delay to learn the gravity of the illness in order that the confessor may prepare the patient to appear before God.

Even when there is no danger it is good to have the confessor visit the sick, were it only to show the interest he takes in the children. It often happens that troubled consciences find peace during a sojourn in the infirmary. If the confessor entered there only in cases of mortal illness his presence might produce a painful sensation.

We should not fear to warn our children of the gravity of their state and of the approach of death. The world seeks to hide from the sick the danger they are in, and, for fear of alarming, leaves them in a fatal illusion. We, on the contrary, taking into account only what tends to the salvation of our children, should tell them, gently and with precaution, the truth as to their condition. Experience has shown that this manner of acting is not at all injurious to the sick.

We should also ask them to whom they

wish to leave what belongs to them; when they have a little money they generally leave it for Masses, we should encourage them to do so. If they have occasion to make a will it is better to have recourse to a lawyer.

We should not forget the families of our children — in most cases a visit would be a mutual consolation. The family should be informed in time, of the gravity of the illness, and after the death of the child, notice should be immediately given, that the friends may assist at the interment. Want of foresight in these matters might lead to much unpleasantness and draw reproach on our houses and on religion.

When a child has received the sacraments — Confession, Communion, and Extreme Unction — she should be left to make her thanksgiving with recollection; her last moments should be soothed by every care spiritual and corporal.

« The greatest temptations the penitents have to endure are usually against faith and hope. Do not cease to strengthen the truths of religion in their souls, and to encourage in them a firm hope in divine mercy. Sometimes when they are near death, if they tell you that they cannot hope to be saved after having contributed to the ruin of so many souls, sustain them, and encourage them to trust in God, by placing before them the proofs we have of His infinite goodness to sinners. » *(Inst.*, ch. XLIX.)

After death, the body shall be laid out with all the care demanded by christian piety, and unless for some grave reason such as rapid decomposition, it should be exposed in a place where the children can pray around it without interruption, and, in order that all may be done religiously, a serious person shall be named to remain near the corpse.

« When we close the eyes of our poor penitents, what a consolation it is for us to think that they will open in eternity to the ineffable beauty of Heaven! They generally depart this life with such great resignation and in such an edifying manner! You, my dear children, who have the merit of helping them to save their souls, will be rewarded, for they that instruct in justice shall shine as stars through all eternity. » *(Inst.*, ch. XXXI.)

CHAPTER XXI

The Lectures

Extreme prudence should be used in the choice of books to be placed in the hands of our children, some of whom might receive an evil impression from books apparently quite harmless. Sentiments which would quickly pass away in the noise of the world are much more persistent in the silent sedentary life of our classes.

The books used, should be, so to say, composed expressly for our children. Certain works written by excellent authors, lives of saints and books of piety, contain details capable of troubling the minds of our children. Reading, very good for other persons, is sometimes injurious to them. Such books may be read in public, care being taken to pass over anything objectionable.

A work might be useful to one child and injurious to another; a good book given at the proper time is a great help to a soul. The children should not be allowed to take the books themselves. A judicious and attentive Mistress can by observation discern what works are most edifying, interesting, and suitable to the different characters, ages, and conditions of her children. A book like a plant does not succeed equally in different countries

In choosing books we should not confine ourselves to those that are simply harmless, we should seek the very best. In the first rank we should place the lives of the Saints. The best books of piety, the best lives of Saints, are those written by Saints. We should prefer works of piety coming from the pen of a priest to those composed by laymen and still more to those written by women.

It is needless to say that a library containing pious books only, would be incomplete. It is most desirable that our children have amusing and recreative lectures. We cannot take too much pains to preserve them from sadness and dullness so prejudicial to the soul.

In preservation classes it is necessary to have books treating in an interesting style, on the discoveries and principal events of our times; otherwise the children brought up in these classes, would, on entering the world, be at a great loss, by their ignorance of things that all are expected to know.

In order to habituate our children to read attentively and with reflection, it is well to question them on what they have read and encourage them to ask explanations of what they do not understand.

To know the nature of a work we should consult a well-informed, disinterested person — our Reverend Chaplains are, in general, the best judges in these matters. We cannot trust implicitly to the appreciations of new works given even in religious periodicals; still less the recommendations of booksellers.

In virtue of a decree of the Holy See, no work treating on religious questions can be published without ecclesiastical approbation and authority [1]. It follows that any work which has not this approbation, should be rejected.

---

[1] « Books and pamphlets of prayers, devotions, doctrine, and moral, religious, ascetic, or mystic teaching, although they appear proper to entertain the piety of the faithful, cannot be published without the permission of legitimate authority, under pain of being prohibited.

« Books and writings giving accounts of new apparitions, revelations, visions, prophecies, new miracles, or

Generally the approbation only assures that a book contains nothing contrary to the teachings of the Church, without guaranteeing its merits — it should be read to be appreciated.

When we consult about a book we should clearly indicate it. It is not sufficient, for instance, to say, the *Life of Saint Francis d'Assise* — we should give the author. The same subject may have been treated by different writers. The lives of Saints have been written sometimes by heretics or by unbelievers. The name of the author is alone sufficient for a well-informed person to judge of the merit of a work.

The above rules apply to the classical books used in our schools, which should be carefully examined lest impiety be hidden in them. We will add that we should encourage good writers by buying their books rather than those of the enemies of religion, who hide their evil sentiments through motives of interest.

---

which suggest new devotions even under pretext that they are private, are forbidden, if they be published without the authorization of ecclesiastical Superiors. » (*Extract from the Constitution apostolic of our Holy Father Pope Leo XIII, on the interdiction of books.*)

CHAPTER XXII

Entrance and Departure

The end of our vocation being the salvation of souls, we ought to rejoice [1] every time a child presents herself for admittance to our class, and receive her with the greatest charity, considering her as sent by God, to be sanctified. Our poor penitents when they arrive, are, in general, crushed and despon-

---

[1] « What woman having ten groats, if she lose one groat, doth not light a candle, and sweep the house, and seek diligently until she find it? And when she hath found it, call together her friends and neighbours saying : " Rejoice with me because I have found the groat which I had lost. " Our groats are our dear penitents. Rejoice at their entrance into the fold, for they are so many groats which were lost and have been found. They were yours, these poor children, even before you knew them. » *(Inst., ch. IV.)*

« I have just learned that In one of our houses they received ten penitents in one day. How many sins will be prevented by means of our dear Sisters! Go, my dear Sisters, go in search of souls to all the countries of the universe. » *(Inst., ch. XLIX.)*

dent or reckless. The best means of bringing them to good, is to make them understand that the past is quite past, that with a new name they are to commence a new life, that they will be judged and esteemed only by their conduct in the house.

« What may not this poor penitent remitted to your hands, become? She may become a true Magdalen, a Thais, a Pelagius. How beautiful is your mission, my beloved children! » *(Inst.,* ch. LIII.)

When a child is presented for admittance we should if possible get her certificate of baptism and know if she made her first communion and received confirmation. We should also make inquiry from the person who recommends her, as to her antecedents, etc., in order to know how to treat this new sheep; but we should never question the child herself on her past life nor let her suspect that we have received any information about her.

In the case of persons who come of their own accord, we should learn the motive of their coming, and, if they be aged, not admit them too easily. There are persons who go about from convent to convent, settling nowhere, but causing disorder wherever they pass. Still, even with these, we should use charity, in the hope of saving their souls.

Persons who place children in our classes, should be requested to specify their intentions with regard to the correspondence these children may have with persons outside, whether by visits or letters. This precaution will spare us many difficulties, we being thus authorized to refuse all communications except those indicated. We should inform them that no visit will be permitted during the first two months unless for some special reason.

All particulars and recommendations concerning each child, with the date of her entry, should be written down as also the address of the persons to whom we could have recourse in case of difficulty and to whom we could give up the child if we find it impossible to keep her.

We should never refuse a penitent because she or her parents cannot pay for her maintenance, but, if they can, we should exact their doing so.

« Our object is to attract penitents; to take, if possible, all who present themselves; to refuse none, however poor they may be.

« And, in truth, it seems as if there was a special Providence for the houses of the Good Shepherd. Frequently they seem to be utterly without resources, yet, they have never wanted for what was necessary; in one way or another God has always helped them. We see this every year in the circular letters. » *(Inst.*, ch. vii.)

In case of a minor, the parents or guardians should sign a contract that she will remain in our class until she shall have attained her majority, and that they will pay a certain fixed sum should she leave before that period. This agreement may have no weight in law, we may be obliged to give up the children when the parents demand them, but it may have the effect of restraining certain persons who would not wish to violate such a promise.

The parents' engagement to leave the child in the house until her majority, does not deprive the Mistress of the right to send her away for grave reasons of which the Mistress and Superioress are the judges.

When a person who is of age enters of her own accord we should also exact an engagement that she will remain at least two years in the house, and that she will pay (provided she has any means) a stated amount if she leave before that time has expired.

Children under age, who ask to enter our classes, should have the written consent of their parents or other persons who have a right over them, or of the civil authorities. This formality is necessary to justify their presence in our house.

Persons who can pay an annual pension, should, when they enter our classes, be obliged to give at least an oral consent to submit to the rule of the house, to work, and to obedience. In reality they shall not be required to work as much as their companions, and if we have agreed to give them better food, of course we must see that they receive it.

As soon as a child enters the enclosure she shall leave off her worldly dress, and care shall be taken that she do not keep possession of the objects she has brought, whether money, rings, papers, photographs, or other things which may be dangerous to her because of the souvenirs attached to them. Her trunk should be examined lest it might contain bad books or papers which should be immediately destroyed.

As has been said in the chapter on *Order*,

all the clothing brought to the house by the children, shall be carefully put aside; the children shall not be allowed to go to their trunks lest they might take the souvenirs stowed away there. If a child prefer using her own linen it shall be given to her but never put in common.

Before being allowed to take her place with the other children the new arrival should be confided to a person on whose devotedness, discretion, and virtue, we can rely, who will watch over her carefully. This is one of the most delicate charges we can give any of our children, we should choose a person of mature age and cheerful disposition, gifted with the tact to amuse and distract. During the first days, new children are fond of talking of the world, of the life they led there, of the persons they knew, etc... Such conversations, by awakening memories that should be effaced, would certainly be dangerous for a curious light-headed person; they should be made to understand that they must try to forget the past. They ought not to be placed in contact with companions they knew in the world, and should be warned not to reveal anything concerning them. Newcomers should never be permitted to go through the house alone. Experience has shown that we cannot exercise too much vigilance in their regard; on the other hand we should not let them suspect that we mistrust them. There are cases when the very presence of a child in a class might cause the gravest trouble. We should take every precaution not to let the wolf enter the fold.

When persons worthy of confidence, make reports about any child, we should lend a willing ear, and if from well-founded information we see that it is impossible to keep her in the house, we shall not delay in taking the measures necessitated by prudence and charity.

The time of trial may be prolonged according to the character and disposition of each new child; when all due precautions have been taken she shall be placed with her companions. It is important that, in the beginning especially, the children be treated with great kindness; otherwise they may take an aversion to the house, and " first impressions are hard to eradicate". The Mistress should speak to them often, to show that she takes an interest in them, but, as has been said, should not question them on their past lives, nor allow them to relate histories which might disturb and which we need not know. If they be sad, some little distractions might be afforded them, even in time of silence, but newcomers who show forwardness should be repressed, and severity used, if necessary, to inspire submission.

« The majority of them have little education, and take pleasure in sin; it is only possible to win them to God by treating them with the utmost delicacy.

« Let us endeavour, then, with gentleness and kindness, to sustain the bruised reed, and let us not extinguish the smoking flax. If we treat with harshness these souls that God Himself has touched by his grace, we have reason to fear that God, in punishment for our temerity and pride, may abandon us to our own strength. » *(Inst.*, ch. XLIX.)

« Beware of too much fault finding; let your manner be grave, but most kind, particularly to our dear penitents who come from the world. For, whatever the source of their tears, they are always very bitter, and if they do not meet with great kindness from you, they may fall into despair.

« Do not let their first dispositions mislead you; frequently, on entering our fold, the first feeling they experience is one of antipathy for the house, and sometimes even for whosoever is charged to guide them; but afterwards, if they be well-treated and surrounded with thoughtful care and marks of interest, they alter, and begin to relish the charm of religion. Then follow, esteem and attachment for the religious, and many of them, as you see, end by wishing never to leave us. » *(Inst.. ch, l.)*

The greater number of our children we know desire to return to the world. The thought that they will be once more exposed to the danger of going astray — and in truth few persevere in the christian practices they had adopted in the good Shepherd — is a sorrow for a Religious. We should then make every effort to induce them to remain in the asylum opened to them by Divine Providence, where they are assured of the grace of a happy death. Our efforts may not be successful in most cases but we will have the consolation of feeling that we did what depended on us [1].

---

[1] « It has been observed that usually there are two kinds of conversion among those poor children. The first is not solid, for they preserve sentiments which

The departure of a penitent is generally a misfortune; it causes as much grief as her arrival caused joy.

There are cases however when we should not try to prevent a child's leaving — for instance, when a young girl who has no attraction for enclosure can return to her family, where, we have reason to believe, she will find no obstacle to her perseverance in virtue.

When any of our children manifest a desire for the religious life and can find admittance into a community, the services she renders and the good influence she exercises around her, are not reasons for opposing her vocation. To prevent her following the call of God would evidently be contrary to her good and happiness; if through motives of interest we endeavoured to retain her we would certainly regret it.

There are, unfortunately, cases in which,

---

change like the seasons. For example, they will be exemplary all during the winter, but on the return of spring you will see that their imagination is disturbed by the memories of what they have left in the world, and they are anxious to return to it..... The second conversion, however, is fruitful, therefore we must not be discouraged, my dear children. » *(Inst.*, ch. XLIX.)

for the general good, we are obliged to send away a child because of the scandal she gives. When every means of reform has failed, we should not fear, to remove one who troubles the order of the class and injures her companions.

It is desirable, sometimes it is necessary, that the Reverend Chaplain be informed of the departure of a child or of her intention to leave.

When a child returns to the world we should give her back everything she brought with her. If she has passed a considerable time in the house, we should reward her services, by providing her with a suitable outfit and a little sum of money — this is not, perhaps, an affair of justice, since our children do not enter our house to earn money, but it is an obligation of charity. To send away a child without clothing or resource, would be to expose her to fall immediately into disorder, and give her cause of resentment against us. Let us be generous to our children — they may perhaps be grateful for it — rather than, by an excess of parsimony, merit complaints they might make against the establishment and which would easily find an echo in the world.

It is evident that those who have been but a short time with us, cannot expect a trousseau on leaving; they have a right to nothing, still we should have them neatly dressed and pay their travelling expenses to their own place.

A child should never be told beforehand, the date of her departure; those thinking of leaving, would give her commissions, and besides, she might yield to dissipation and thus cause trouble in the class.

When about to leave, those who have come from a distance, sometimes give very plausible reasons for wishing to remain in town — their real motive being, to await a companion with whom they have formed some project: this is often the beginning of a new life of sin. Unless we have been able to find them a situation, we should send them back to the place they came from, have them accompanied to the station by a tourière Sister who should take their tickets, choose a carriage where they will be in safe company, and wait until the train starts. Children who are unaccustomed to travel, should be recommended to the guard or some other person worthy of confidence. Parents or others interested, should be informed of our intention of sending a child away, and also of the exact hour at which they may expect her at her destination. By thus getting due notice, the friends may, if they wish, procure for her a situation.

If we could provide our children with situations at an easy distance from the convent, we might perhaps be able to sustain them in their good dispositions. We should of course do all that depends on us to enable our children to earn their bread honestly, but we should not recommend children whose misconduct would be sure to bring discredit on the house and prevent our being able to help others who merit protection. Besides, we should not deceive persons who would accept them on our recommendation.

It is important that children who come to see us, after having returned to the world, be well received and welcomed. By this means we may continue our ascendancy over them, give them good advice, strengthen their resolutions, or bring them back to the path of duty if they have strayed from it. In their misfortunes they will have recourse to us and we may again be the instruments of grace in their regard.

Many children who have left the Good Shepherd, ask to return. If we can take them back we ought not to miss this opportunity of saving them, we ought to welcome the poor stray sheep who return to the fold although it is not from them we can expect most consolation. If for some particular reason they cannot be admitted into the house they quitted, we might try to place them in another. We should more willingly take back those who have been withdrawn by their parents, contrary to their own will.

If it were possible to have homes wherein our children could pass some time before being sent to situations, and to which they could return when out of place, we would have a better chance of assuring their perseverance. A sojourn in an intermediate class would enable children (who being brought up in our classes, were accustomed to be watched over by their Mistresses and led by the example of their companions) to acquire some knowledge of the world and use of their liberty before being entirely thrown on their own resources. Children obliged to leave their situation could find in this home a shelter from danger while awaiting another place. Finally, our young girls living in or near town, could be invited to spend a few hours there on Sundays and holidays. Some of our convents have experienced the many advantages of such a supplement to our classes.

For young girls who leave our *Grande Classe*, (penitents) such a home would not be less useful, although perhaps, more difficult. In fact it is almost the only means by which we could hope to obtain the dear children's perseverance, as by it we could continue to exercise our influence over them and help them to be faithful to their duty. It is rare indeed that these poor children when left to contend with the world, do not return to their old habits. We should do all in our power not to lose sight of them when they leave our class; our solicitude should follow them in the world and aid them in being faithful.

CHAPTER XXIII

Order and cleanliness

It is most important, from every point of view, that our children be trained to habits of order and cleanliness. The Mistresses should on all occasions give them the example of these two qualities, we might almost say, virtues. « In our establishments, perfect order should reign. It is evident at a first glance whether order reigns in a class or not. » *(Inst.*, ch. L.)

The religious should be always neat and clean, their clothes never torn or negligently put on. Certain saints, carried away by penitential fervor, have cast aside habits of cleanliness; they would not have done so, if they had had to live amongst our children and form them by their example.

Everything in our service should be perfectly clean; when we have finished using a thing, we should immediately put it in its place.

This recommendation is important, not only with a view to neatness but also to save time which would be lost arranging our things, or looking for them when wanted.

The children's clothing should be kept in perfect order. « Our young girls are offended if they see the contrary, although they are sometimes disorder itself. *(Inst.*, ch. L.)

The Mistress should see that order is observed in the different employments, and should never suffer the children to be dirty in person or untidy in dress: their hair should be well-combed « Let your children be very neat and their clothes carefully mended. » *(Inst.*, ch. L.)

They should not be allowed, at recreation, to drag or push each other, to throw themselves on the ground, or leave their work in the dust.

To encourage them to be careful of their clothes and of everything in their use, a recompense might be promised to those who preserve them best, for instance, a good note or a little prize when they return them.

The class-room, dormitories, refectory, yard, etc. should be regularly swept and the furniture dusted.

Needless to say, that the chapel and everything pertaining to divine worship should be specially and religiously attended to. We might easily scandalize our children by carelessness about holy things, by having pictures or statues dusty, the altars without ornaments, or by neglecting what may tend to excite piety.

The first Mistress should keep her account books [1] in order. She should endeavour to be prompt with her payments and take every precaution against contracting debts, by calculating the resources at her disposal for the use of the class, and not allowing her expenses to exceed them. The books should be kept in such a way that if the Mistress died suddenly, or were changed, the Sister succeeding her, could, on consulting them, learn the financial state of the class.

It is advisable that the first Mistress draw up a *Coutumier* in which she might mark down the different events that take place in the class, the customs introduced, the motives

---

[1] « Mistresses of class should also have their account books, for they should render an exact account of their expenses, to the Superior. » *(Inst.,* ch. LV.)

for taking such a measure, etc. These notes would be useful to her successors. A Religious should not work for herself alone, she should think of the future; the class she is directing will survive her, it is just that she take every means to make it prosper even when she is gone. A father thinks of the future of his family; a religious is a Mother, she cannot be without interest in the children who are to come after her.

Each child's papers as also the notes the Mistress takes at her entry and departure, should be carefully locked past. These notes are often necessary, even when children have left our house.

The clothing and other articles belonging to a child, should be put aside in such a manner that they can be easily found and returned in case of her sudden and unforeseen departure.

The children sometimes bring some money which they deposit in the hands of the Mistress. Such sums should be kept apart, so that they can be given back at any moment.

When a person gives money for the use of a child it should be employed for her only — the same may be said of provisions or other things; they should not be put in common, or given to several.

What is given for a class ought to be employed for the benefit of that class, over and above what it receives from the community — of course this does not apply to donations made to help the house rather than to procure *extras* for the children.

CHAPTER XXIV

Discernment or the Study of Characters

« Observe, my dear children, that what may serve to convert one penitent, may have a contrary effect on another. Great discernment is required to speak opportunely. » *(Inst.,* ch. LI.)

Each child has her own character which must be studied. In imitation of the Good Shepherd we must try *to know our sheep* — *by* observing them, listening to them, learning the opinion formed of them by persons who have known them for some time, and by observing how these persons treat them. We should avoid acting with precipitation or in a uniform manner, and keep in view the general good of the class without losing sight of the particular interest of each soul, taking into account our own observations and the remarks communicated to us by others.

These principles have inspired many of the rules indicated in this little book. In the chapter on *Authority* it was shown that kindness has little effect on children who have not much heart, they must be treated rather severely. In the chapter on *Justice* it has been remarked, that we should not under pretext of equality and justice, adopt a uniform treatment at the risk of causing discouragement or rebellion. It is true that, as regards *punishments*, we ought to hold rigorously to what has been established, but it is not less true, that penalties should be proportioned to culpability, and our judgment of the latter, is, in a great measure, determined by our knowledge of the habitual dispositions of a child; it is also by considering her general character, that we can decide whether the punishment ought to be tiresome or humiliating, grave or light, or whether it would be more profitable to reason with the culprit or take no notice of her. On *Work*, *Silence*, etc. — it has been seen that the same exterior failings do not, in different children, proceed from the same defect of character and could not be corrected by the same means. We will add here some remarks on certain characters particularly difficult to govern, followed by a few observations on differences of disposition, resulting from the age of the children or local influences.

We sometimes meet with children sincerely desirous to correct themselves, although they often fall into serious faults; for such, remonstrance kindly and calmly administered or a slight penance, is the best means of correction.

The same manner of acting would be a subject of derision and an encouragement to evil-doing if used towards those who have made up their minds, not to improve. Amongst the latter there are bold forward girls who think they can overcome everyone by their boisterous manner — a severe reprimand given cooly and briefly in public, will subdue them. They should be treated with unflinching severity, sometimes it is better to show indifference or contempt for their conduct.

Proud persons, particularly if they be *very sensitive* and not very generous in overcoming themselves, have a great repugnance to asking pardon for their faults; it is often better not to oblige them to it. The slightest mark of contempt drives such persons to revolt and leads to great disorder. They are more easily touched by being shown that their faults render their good qualities useless. We might appeal to their self-love as a motive for repentance but in this, much tact is required, in order not to flatter and encourage their pride, particularly if this vice were the cause of the faults we are reprehending.

We should rarely reprimand in public those who are very *susceptible*, but never to reprehend them would be weakness on our part and an encouragement to their susceptibility; it might cause others to imitate their conduct.

Public reprimands are generally unprofitable. The person to whom they are addressed, is, through human respect, irritated, and will not acknowledge her fault; some who have a bad spirit enjoy the thought that more than one of their companions approve their resistance. When reproved in private a child more easily admits she is wrong and is more disposed to profit of the caution and advice given her.

In some cases we may use public reprimands [1] for the general good or to make a

---

[1] « If too frequent reprimands are an abuse, the absence of all reprimands is no less an error. There are times when it is absolutely necessary to make our authority felt. I was once obliged to speak very severely to a penitent whose conduct at first seemed very exemplary, but who afterwards scandalized her companions as much as she had edified them. Nothing seemed

child ashamed by humbling her pride —
if it be not too violent, — but we must be very
reserved. A Mistress gifted with natural wit
might be proud to make some clever strokes,
but if her witty remarks ever wound the
children's self-love she will have cause to
repent them : wounds thus inflicted are
sometimes incurable. We should be particularly careful not to use, when reprimanding a
child in public, reproaches that might be
applied to all : to say, for instance. « I could
expect no better. It is only through charity
I occupy myself with you. » We should rather
try to raise the children in their own esteem
by saying. « I am surprised you act so, I am
sure your companions are quite ashamed of
your conduct. »

We should avoid reproving often in public,
timid children or those inclined to *sadness* or
discouragement. It might have the effect of
developing in them an unhealthy feeling of
envy or vindictiveness. The same remark
applies to awkward unintelligent children ; if

---

capable of making her seriously consider her faults. A
humiliation finally conquered her, and brought her back
to duty. But severe measures like these must be only
rarely employed. » *(Inst.,* ch. LII.)

too much notice were taken of their defects, or if their companions were allowed to mock them, it would cause them much pain : we should be very kind to them.

We should seize every opportunity to encourage the children by congratulating them when they show good-will or obtain a little success. It is sometimes wise to let them believe they have a virtue a quality or an aptitude when it is only beginning to appear: that may create in them a love for it and make them endeavour to acquire it, but we must not go too far and humiliate a child by admiring in her what is quite ordinary in others.

Persons inclined to anger should be treated with gentleness and firmness. A hasty word is sufficient to arouse their passion.

When a child is angry or ill-disposed, is not the time to impose a penance on her nor even to try to make her obey — her good sentiments are then paralized and her reason obscured. We must await a more favourable moment, lest we drive the child to more obstinate resistance which would aggravate her fault while diminishing our authority.

As to *self-willed* persons — we should avoid giving them a direct order when we have reason to fear they would not submit to it, neither should we try to make them yield when they have refused to do a thing, our insisting would have the same result in their case as in that of persons in a passion.

« Be very prudent, my dear daughters, and do not expose yourselves to being disobeyed and treated with disrespect. » *(Inst.*, ch. L.)

We sometimes meet with *bad natures* in which no good sentiment can be awakened. They spread around them corruption and revolt; sometimes joining perfidy to their other defects they succeed for a time in deceiving everybody by an appearance of virtue. Such persons are capable of acquiring a certain influence of which they make use to lead their less intelligent companions into faults; they prevent good, cause much sin, and destroy the spirit of a class. As soon as discovered they should be dismissed; they will do less harm in the world than in our houses; we could never hope to convert them unless they be very young and that the Mistress clearly detects their evil dispositions. When informing the parents or other persons who have confided these children to us, of our intention of sending them away, we should say as little as possible against them and express our regret at being obliged to come to this resolution.

In general when we have to complain of children to their parents or guardians we should use mild terms, having regard for their feelings and avoiding as far as possible what could wound them. People of the world easily complain of want of charity in religious; we should give them no cause to do so.

Aged persons, no matter what defects they may have, should be treated with kindness and forbearance particularly if they have spent many years in the house. They may have rendered great services in their younger days and it is only just that we do all in our power to make more supportable a life which in many ways must be very painful at their advanced years. If the young penitents see the ancient ones unhappy they will not attach themselves to the house, on the contrary, they will be anxious to leave while yet young. If we should be kind to the young in order to encourage them we are still more obliged to be kind to the aged, taking into account their infirmities, not over working them, procuring them little comforts and not reprimanding them before their young companions unless for a public fault which our silence would seem to excuse too much.

It may be said of classes as of children, each has its own particular character which should be observed and studied and never lost sight of — a manner of acting, excellent in one house, might be quite unsuited to another. In two classes of penitents the general spirit may differ widely, such disparity being probably caused by difference in the children's origin or by local circumstances. It is therefore important when we change from one class to another, to bend without delay to the necessities of the situation. It sometimes requires the exercise of great self-renunciation and much virtue to give up a method which one has been following for years, and which has, so to say, become part of herself.

Characters vary with countries — they are not the same in America as in Europe, there is sometimes a marked difference of character and temperament between Northerns and Southerns of the same country. When a Sister changes from one foundation to another she has much to learn, and in such matters, nothing can supply for personal experience, but while waiting to acquire it, she can make use of the experience of others [1].

« St Basil and with him all the Doctors say that prudence consists in a just discernment of what one must do and what one must not do, according to the various circumstances in which we are placed. " Let thine eyes look straight on, " says the wise man, " and let thine eyelids go before thy steps ". Do nothing without reflection or a pure and upright intention. They who act lightly and without reflection end by falling over a precipice. It is said that he who would live wisely must live a life of reflection. » *(Inst.*, ch. XLI)

---

[1] « One thing we should specially guard against, is, yielding to prejudiced, unfavourable impressions of any of our monasteries, or of any country whatever. » *(Inst.*, ch. XXXI.)

CHAPTER XXV

Discretion

Discretion obliges a religious to be extremely reserved with the children. Never should she speak to them of herself, the name she bore in the world, of her family or country, nor should she show them portraits or letters of her friends, parade what she knows, or speak to them of what is said and done in the community. Our Venerable Mother Foundress recommended great discretion on points these.

The Mistresses should never question the children about their past life, nor permit them to reveal secrets of conscience which regard only the confessor.

They should not interrogate a child on the faults of her companions unless she be charged with some employment of surveillance.

We may remark in passing, that, unfortunately, we sometimes meet in our penitent and preservation classes, children who are naturally inclined to be deceitful or untruthful. We must do all in our power to counteract this tendency — but, never shall we succeed unless we ourselves, by word and act, give the example of straightforwardness and truth. That will not prevent our concealing scrupulously facts which should not be revealed. We should never, without necessity, speak of the children's faults or of their family affairs. Like true Mothers we ought to uphold the reputation of our children.

We should never ask a child for anything and, as a general rule, accept nothing from her; however a Mistress may take pictures on her feast-day. No Sister can give or lend things belonging to the class, without the authorization of the first Mistress.

We should not touch the children nor allow them to touch even our clothes, still less should we allow them to embrace us. A Religious could not be too strict on these points which are of extreme importance.

The Religious of the Good Shepherd should always observe the most perfect modesty in her conversation, looks, manner, etc.

It will be profitable to read the following recommendations of our Venerable Mother Foundress.

« Be particularly prudent in your intercourse with our dear penitents and others; for example, if you are about to leave a class and be sent elsewhere, it would not be prudent on your part to appear in their midst with tearful swollen eyes, and take your leave of them, saying with a sigh. " I will do the will of God ; I abandon myself to His providence " and other similar expressions of resignation, which would probably only excite and disorganize the class. » *(Inst.,* ch. XLI.)

« Let me warn you my dear children, you who are employed with the penitents and Magdalens and the children of the various classes, to beware of ever being familiar with them ; never speak to them even of your health : you may be sure that any want of dignity on your part will unfit you to be their Mistress. It would be very unseemly for a religious to speak of herself, of her family, or of what she was in the world. It would be still more unseemly for a Mistress to confide to the children the trials and difficulties she may encounter. This would not only be petty, but she would risk losing the respect which every one consecrated to God should command by the dignity of her conduct. » *(Inst.,* ch. L.)

CHAPTER XXVI

Patience

A Religious of the Good Shepherd, gifted though she may be with the most precious qualities and animated by the best intentions, will realize the hopes founded on her, only on condition that she be truly patient. « To succeed in saving souls we must know how to suffer and bear many privations and pain. We must have great patience with our poor children. » *(Inst.*, ch. xxv.)

The trials awaiting us in our mission are sometimes very heavy; it is important that we never let ourselves be irritated or cast down by them. Whatever may happen, we must remain Mistress of ourselves, of our actions, of our words, and even of our sentiments. Tribulation should not raise a tempest in our soul; in the midst of exterior opposition peace and calm must dwell within us.

Words spoken or measures taken in a

moment of agitation, are almost always regrettable. An unjust or humiliating word uttered through impatience is sometimes sufficient to irritate or discourage a child for life.

Patience will enable us to support without complaining and without disgust the defects of our children. If we listened only to the suggestions of nature, we would sometimes feel inclined to rid ourselves of a person, who, notwithstanding the kindness and charity lavished in her regard, makes no effort to improve. Let us take for our model, God who while patiently awaiting the sinner's repentance, puts no limit to His grace and mercy. Let us multiply our sacrifices, hoping against hope that the hour of grace will strike at last and that God will bless our efforts. Let us not say that a child is incorrigible and that it is useless to work for her conversion — such would be the language of discouragement and indolence [1].

If we were not vigilant to repress every movement of impatience we would soon be

---

[1] In the case of a child who corrupts her companions she should be treated as has been said in ch. xxiv.

unable to bear anything, and consequently, being no longer Mistress of our temper, we could not teach our children to overcome themselves; they would quickly remark the striking opposition between our preaching and our practice. At the same time we would become almost incapable of acting with prudence — for, how study characters and reflect on the means of directing them with justice and kindness, when the soul is violently agitated, filled with tumult and looking at things through the magnifying glass of discontent or melancholy?

« Melancholy, taciturn virtue, harsh, hard virtue (which is only virtue in name) is not inspired by the spirit of God, and does not become a christian soul, much less a Religious of the Good Shepherd. » *(Inst.,* ch. xv.)

It is necessary, for the salvation of souls, that we acquire entire command over self, and that, sustained by zeal, we shrink from no effort to obtain unalterable patience. We must endeavour to become impassable, and capable of bearing with calmness of soul and serenity of countenance, the different impressions caused by fatigue, illness, weariness, annoyances, and failure.

We must not be susceptible, ready to feel mortified and to complain of words and actions which were not meant to be offensive. Susceptibility is one of the defects against which we must be most carefully on our guard; it causes errors and injustices without number and engenders a sadness as disastrous as vain; and yet, susceptible persons with great difficulty see or acknowledge their defect when it is pointed out to them.

When the conduct of the children is really afflicting we must try not to show our feelings, at least not to be angry. Perverse children aim simply at annoying their Mistresses and putting them out of temper; if they succeed, it is an encouragement to continue, whilst if they fail they resign themselves to be quiet. In the first case they feel themselves stronger than we and our authority is diminished, in the second, they conceive a higher idea of our character, and respect us the more.

By pretending not to notice a word or act intended to irritate us, we disappoint the person who sought to distinguish herself by public insubordination and contempt for authority, whereas by a contrary mode of action, we would draw the attention of the entire class to the fault, and would perhaps cause general dissipation, besides exposing ourselves to public humiliation.

Those who yield to impatience, often say hasty words contrary to their real sentiments, and thereby irritate and offend the children.

Some persons cannot wait — once they have taken a determination it must be immediately carried into effect. When they are ready everyone must be ready. Supernatural zeal is more calm and thoughtful; it can brook the delay required by wisdom. Hasty persons should correct their impetuosity and acquire the virtue of patience so necessary for every one in authority. For this end they should never lose sight of the divine *Crucified*. They must consider as did all the Saints, that without suffering, detachment from self nor union with God can never be obtained; that souls cannot be saved without suffering; that to participate in the redeeming mission of the Good Shepherd, we must have a share in His sufferings physical and moral.

Let us not be surprised when we meet with some great affliction; let us rather bless the Lord for having deigned to render us like to Himself and for having associated us to His work in a manner so efficacious. In the midst of our tribulations we will find consolation in the thought that we are contributing to the salvation of the souls we love.

« We must know how to patiently endure crosses, humiliations, contradictions, if we would draw upon ourselves and our Institute the blessings of Heaven.

« I was very sensitive at one time to contradictions, particularly to those which came to us through certain persons; they troubled me. Now, my soul is equally tranquil under all circumstances. At Rome, when I thought of the catacombs which contain the bones of the martyrs, that horrible cavern into which the Apostles descended through a narrow opening, that Coliseum, amphitheatre where so many generous souls suffered such cruel torments, I said to myself, what are our sufferings, what are our tribulations, compared to such tortures? Then let us suffer, let us suffer in union with the Church, which has always had to endure calumnies, tribulations, persécutions!

« By suffering, by zeal, by prayer, and close union with the Church militant, you will relieve the suffering Church, and you will smooth the way to becoming (were it even by martyrdom), a part of the Church triumphant. What is more, my dear daughters, by the crosses which you will have generously borne, holding firmly to the faithful observance of all that is prescribed you in our holy Constitutions, in our Directory, and our Spiritual Exercises, you will have the honor to be regarded almost as so many martyrs. Then be very fervent. God has great designs upon each one of you. Ask him to grant you His love, the love of souls, and you will see what marvels this holy love will effect in you. *(Inst.,* ch. III.)

CHAPTER XXVII

For Classes of Young Children

The training of children should be regarded as a work of the utmost importance and nothing should be left undone to prepare them for the « Battle of Life » in which they must engage later on.

It has been remarked that girls who have been brought up in Convents, removed from all evil associations, and carefully instructed in their religious duties, are sometimes found less able to cope with the difficulties of the world, than others who have been brought up in perhaps very indifferent homes. This arises in a great measure from their want of experience in the world's ways. As a precaution against this evil it would be well to arrange the present duties of the children with a view to their future requirements, both as regards their spiritual duties and their employments.

Train them to make with fervour the morning offering of the Apostleship of Prayer in which all should be enrolled. This devotion of the Apostleship of Prayer has been found most efficacious, without punishment, in training the children to habits of virtue. The Treasury Sheet encourages them to practise an incredible number of acts of obedience, self-denial, charity, and to devote themselves to prayer, work, and study. Being thus habituated to watch over themselves in childhood, a check is placed on their evil propensities in later years.

The morning and night prayers should be very carefully said, but so short that the omission of them afterwards could not be excused by want of time. Extra prayers should be said when the morning are quite finished or at other times.

Teach the children to make occasional aspirations during the day, to be in the Chapel before the Holy Mass commences and to practise some special devotion on the eve of Holy Communion. Urgently impress on them the absolute necessity of Monthly Confession, and so accustom them to this practice from their childhood, that it will become a fixed idea in their future lives.

If these matters be insisted upon, much is accomplished towards the children's salvation.

Truth must be strictly inculcated and every means employed to render the children straight-forward. Should a child acknowledge that she has committed a fault or caused an injury of any kind, she should be at once pardoned and pleasure expressed at her straight-forwardness. It is painful to see a timid child in abject terror at the breaking of a needle, or some such trifle, and through fear of punishment, ready to descend to any meanness, even to the replacing of it by theft. The children should be taught to overcome human respect and not to be afraid to give a candid answer when called on to do so. It is absolutely necessary for them to acquire a certain firmness of character and a courage which will enable them to withstand the temptations to which they will be exposed when thrown on their own responsibility without guidance or protection. The grown girls, sometimes almost unconciously, train the little ones into habits of deceit, by making them pretend for instance, that they are delighted to see a Nun for whom they do not feel the least affection, or that they like Mother

Superior or the first Mistress best; when their feelings are quite the contrary. The little ones must not be continually checked and taught to conceal their ideas; by drawing them out, a knowledge of their character can be obtained and their ideas given a right direction. While many faults may be passed over without punishment, lies or deceit should never.

The grown girls should not be allowed to pet and caress the little ones too much, nor to dress them like dolls with ribbons, lace, etc. That has the effect of weakening character and developing sensibility and vanity. It is essential that our children be strong and self-reliant.

The Sisters must be most careful never to say or do anything in presence of the children, which savours of duplicity even in the least degree, such as, concealing anything when the Mother Superior visits the class, or putting a work aside because the Inspector is expected, etc. The importance of honesty in matters great and small must be frequently explained to the children, and that without permission, they must not appropriate any trifles which they may find about. Employers have been frequently known to place small sums of money and other things in out of the way places in order to test the honesty of their servants. The children should be made to understand how wrong it is to read letters not intended for them, to examine parcels, dresses, drawers, etc., through curiosity, or to pry in any way into the private affairs of others; these propensities if not checked in childhood afterwards result in most pernicious effects. They must be made to understand very forcibly that no girl will be trusted or valued who is not strictly truthful, honest, and honourable.

Obedience and respect to Superiors must be enforced, remembering that, as a rule, the children of our classes have to look forward to lives of dependence and submission, therefore they must be early accustomed to obey without hesitation or murmuring.

The fewer restraints that are placed on the children, the more effectual they will be.

Day after day insist on certain directions being followed, until the children will fully realize that they must obey. Frequently change their employments, sometimes giving them those they least expect; this is a most useful method of training them to obedience and one which will prove of great utility to them amidst the varied occupations of their after lives.

The children should not be encouraged to talk of the faults of their companions; this engenders a spirit of uncharitableness and mischief — making which by becoming habitual renders them, in after years, the pests of society. It should be borne in mind that the children are with us only for a time and that on leaving the school the incidents of their school — days form the principal subject of their conversation. Nothing then should be said or done in their presence which one would not wish to have spoken of to seculars often to those who are not of our Faith. To act otherwise would be to run the risk of giving scandal or at least of impressing seculars with a very low idea of Religious life.

Sisters going among the children for the first time should start with the resolution. — « Never to be off one's guard. » This reserve should not render the Sisters disagreeable or harsh towards the children — on the contrary, they should study how to promote cheerfulness and should do all in their power to render the life of God's little ones bright and happy. Many sorrows may, alas! cloud their future, let them look back to a happy Childhood passed in the peaceful home of their early days — these memories will soften sorrow and draw them near to God.

To ensure respect, the Sisters must carefully avoid in word, manner, and conduct, everything which could give the least disedification. No amount of reasoning can persuade a child to respect one who has shown herself unworthy of it.

As a life of labour is the allotted portion of our children, they should be early accustomed to habits of industry, thrift, and economy. Whatever would prove useful to them in the future must be carefully attended to. The Sisters who have charge of any particular work, should see that it is properly done, and done in the manner that would be required had the children to earn their own livelihood by it.

The very small children who are too young to follow the regular duties, could be occupied at some work at once useful and healthful, such as, helping to weed the gardens, pick up little stones, etc., and should not be allowed to roll on the ground, or soil their clothes. If it be not convenient to have a Sister specially charged with those little ones they should be confided to a grown girl worthy of this confidence. The Mistress should be sure that they be not beaten or *pinched*, and should herself see that they be properly combed and washed. It would be well to give them a bath every week — oftener in warm climates.

A dull, lazy, untidy child must not be cast aside as good for nothing — on the contrary, extra trouble must be taken to train her, knowing that if she be not capable of earning a respectable living she will probably go to destruction. The children should be trained to do their work quickly. If several are employed together in any kind of housework, they should not be allowed to stand idly talking, looking out of the windows, loitering about, etc., but should be made to finish off what they have to do in a quick, clean, orderly manner. They should be put through the various employments that will afterwards be required of them and this even at an inconvenience — always bearing in mind that the future good of the children must be consulted in preference to any personal considerations of the present time. In schools under Government where payment is given for the maintenance of the children, the regulations imposed by the authorities should be conscientiously carried out.

The children should not get ideas beyoud their position in life, but should be taught how to fulfill that position in the most perfect manner possible. They should be taught to mend their clothes, knit their own stockings, cut out, and make their outfits before leaving the school.

The dangers to which they are likely to be exposed when entering on their new life, should be clearly explained to them, they should be particularly warned against making acquaintance with persons of whom they know little or nothing — this explanation is absolutely necessary in countries where girls are allowed great freedom. It is much needed by our children who have been reared in an atmosphere of innocence.

Each child should be carefully warned against her particular failing; a child may have inherited a weakness of which (or at least of its consequences) she is unconsious; if put on her guard she will be armed to combat it. She should be also warned against novels and forcibly recommended to render account of her recreations, etc., to her Confessor when she be at a distance from her Mothers.

The above recommendations are particularly intended, as has been said, for children who will have to earn their livelihood but it can be seen that almost all could be useful in boarding-schools. Our Sisters in charge of young lady boarders, should neglect nothing to advance the education of their pupils, to train them to refinement and polite manners, but they should carefully inculcate habits of industry and economy as most efficient preservatives against many dangers and temptations. Any tendency to vanity, arrogance, or pedantry, should be carefully corrected. Boarders, as well as poor children, should be taught plain sewing and mending; the Mistress should show more appreciation for such work than for fancy work. It is also most desirable to give them some practical knowledge of house-keeping.

They should be formed to self-denial and to practical charity. They could be encouraged, for instance, to deprive themselves of dessert or sweets and as a recompense for good conduct be allowed to distribute them to the orphans or poor children.

Children of every class should be deeply impressed with the idea that piety, virtue, and good sense, are the qualities most prized by all; that without them, accomplishments are little valued even by the world. Above all, that the salvation of their souls is the only real object in this life to which they should aim. Consequently more attention should be paid to their religious training than to all else.

Thus Sisters who by force of circumstances are obliged to occupy themselves with the education of the rich, will have the consolation of feeling that they are labouring for the salvation of souls as well as those who devote themselves to the poor.

God be Blessed!

FIN

CONTENTS

	Pages
Letter of our very honored Mother Mary of Saint Marine	III
Preface	IX
Ch. I. — Zeal	1
Ch. II. — Our own sanctification	4
Ch. III. — To pray for our children	10
Ch. IV — Religious Instructions	13
Ch. V. — Prayers and Devotions	27
Ch. VI. — The Sacraments	41
I. — Observations for the Confessions	42
II. — Observations on the Communion	47
Ch. VII. — Devotedness in our employments	52
Ch. VIII. — The First Mistress	58
Ch. IX. — The Second Mistress and other Sisters employed in the class	78
Ch. X. — Authority, the means of acquiring and preserving it	85
Ch. XI. — Observance of the Rule	94
Ch. XII. — Charity towards the children	97
Ch. XIII. — Justice	102

CONTENTS

Ch. XIV. — Punishments and Rewards....... 109
   I. — Punishments....................... 110
   II. — Recompenses...................... 117
Ch. XV. — Work 121
Ch. XVI. — Silence......................... 129
Ch. XVII. — The Recreations............... 135
Ch. XVIII. — The Meals 144
   I. — Advice to the Sister who serves the children............................. 147
   II. — Advice to the Sister charged with the surveillance during the meals... 150
Ch. XIX. — The Dormitory.................. 152
Ch. XX. — The Infirmary 159
Ch. XXI. — The Lectures 170
Ch. XXII. — Entrance and Departure........ 174
Ch. XXIII. — Order and Cleanliness.......... 189
Ch. XXIV. — Discernment or the Study of Characters 194
Ch. XXV. — Discretion 204
Ch. XXVI. — Patience....................... 207
Ch. XXVII. — For Classes of Young children 214

ANGERS, IMP. LECOQ

www.ingramcontent.com/pod-product-compliance
Lightning Source LLC
Chambersburg PA
CBHW021806230426
43669CB00008B/648